Praise for *Building an Innovative Learning Organization*

"To survive and succeed in today's turbo-charged environment, organizations must not only learn, but innovatively learn. Sarder's book incorporates the best ideas of organizational leaders from around the world and skillfully crafts them into a highly practical narrative that guides and enables readers to build their own innovative learning organizations. This book will soon become a classic in the organizational learning arena."

—**Dr. Michael Marquardt**, President of the World Institute for Action Learning, Professor at George Washington University, and author of 25 bestselling books including *Building the Learning Organization* and *Leading with Questions*

"Learning with and from others has always delivered optimal value for me. *Building an Innovative Learning Organization* takes the best experiences and expertise from leading practitioners and makes them available to everyone. The content of this book encompasses hundreds of years of valuable insights from successful leaders who have not only built highly successful learning organizations, but have been able to enhance and sustain them through complex, turbulent times. Reading this book will deliver similar if not more benefit than the opportunity to network with some of the best minds in the learning field. You owe it to yourself to include this on your upcoming reading list."

—**Karen Kocher**, Chief Learning Officer at Cigna

"Competitive advantage on the business landscape takes many forms. Thought leaders have argued that it is innovation, while others argue it is leadership. Irrespective of the form of competitive advantage that you believe in, there is a singular powerful source for it. The true heartbeat of competitive advantage is learning. Learning as catalyst to competitive advantage is not simply the acquisition of knowledge. It is the ability to *live the learning* in real time, apply that learning to drive exceptional performance and then to teach that application to the rest of the organization. This caliber of organizational learning is sustainable and saleable. When an organization can do this with unconscious competence, they are poised to win. Russell Sarder, our most passionate CEO of Learning, understands this because he has *lived it* as a lifelong learner in his business and in his life. His new book, *Building an Innovative Learning Organization*, takes us deep into the heartbeat of learning to deliver greater value for our businesses while we grow greater value within ourselves by *living the learning*. Sarder is a radical learner and a profoundly passionate teacher on an epic learning journey. Join him. Your learning will never be the same and your competitive advantage will have an invincible heartbeat."

—**Roseanna DeMaria**, Former Chief Learning Office
at Merrill Lynch and Former CLO at NYU SCPS
Leadership & Human Capital Management

"Sarder's point of view on the connection between learning, innovation, and business reinvention is a must-read for business leaders. His research and conclusions make a compelling argument for lifelong learning for both individuals and organizations. Bravo!"

—**David DeFilippo, EdD**, Former CLO of BNY Mellon

"Building a learning organization requires enormous changes for individuals, processes, and culture. Succeeding in this challenging venture requires passion, intelligence, and insight. Those three qualities are illustrated abundantly and painstakingly in Russell Sarder's valuable guide, which makes good use of his hard-earned experience."

—**T.J. Elliott**, Chief Learning Officer at
Education Testing Service (ETS)

"Is the light on? Is anyone at home? As the book cover symbolizes, leaders at all levels need to be alert and aware that learning will keep them from losing in today's global ever-changing economy. Blockbuster and Circuit City didn't learn—and are no more. Learning is no longer a nice-to-have benefit, it is a must-have business skill needed at all levels in the organization. Good ideas can come from anywhere and anyone, and in the globalized economy, all ideas and perspectives are needed. To a coherent overview of the technologies and real business challenges which leaders need to embrace, Russell Sarder adds structures for building a true learning organization, based on his own experience with NetCom Learning, where he is walking the talk. Read this book. Be sure your own light is on, be sure all the people in your organization are aware of the necessity of learning for success, and your organization has the opportunity to live on into the future."

—**Robert M. Burnside**, Partner and
Chief Learning Officer, Ketchum

"*Innovation. Learning. Leadership.* These are powerful words too often rendered vapid by their manipulation and commodification, terms that are overused in rhetoric and underrepresented in reality. Yet, in my interactions with Russell Sarder—in his words, his teachings, his guidance, his mentorship—I have come to observe a man who not only pays lip-service to the notion of building a thriving learning organization but does the work himself every single day, modeling by his actions what that looks like and what is still possible. His newest book, *Building an Innovative Learning Organization*, is culled from his years of experience 'walking the talk,' helping those of us committed to the ideal of lifelong learning become more productive, thoughtful, inspiring, and ultimately more successful leaders. He aspires every day to devour every morsel of knowledge and wisdom available to him, and this book represents yet another effort to ensure that his commitment to learning is not simply self-interested but is shared with those around him to build better businesses, better lives, and hopefully, a better world."

—**Daniel Meyer**, EdM, CLO of
Academica Virtual Education

"I am extremely excited that Russell took the time to write book on such an important topic. By drawing on his own experience in building NetCom Learning as well as the 150 Sarder TV interviews and beyond, he offers curious readers highly practical and interesting principles coupled with strong stories. His framework on how to build a learning organization resonates with my experience and certainly that of BRAC. BRAC, which was dubbed a learning organization in the 1980s, is proud to be a partner of Russell's, and I was honored to be part of Sarder TV. I applaud his initiative!"

—**Susan Davis**, Founder, President,
and CEO at BRAC USA

"Innovative people are dreamers, at odds with the unspoken dictum of so many companies that 'it is better to do nothing than to do something wrong.' Innovative, creative people do what our first-grade teachers warned us not to do, draw outside the box. They look upon organizations like a field just snowed on where every action can leave a visible mark. They embrace change and often risk failure. They are invested in continuous learning and lessons learned. [But] public, private, and government organizations all too often frown upon their ideas. [Yet] organizations that adopt the mantra of education and learning, 'dreamers, seekers, explorers are all welcome here,' are positioned for growth. For without continuous innovation and learning organizations are doomed to stagnation and ultimately failure. A challenge in this century is how to learn from our innovations. Russell explores these issues in an eloquent and innovative way and encourages us to draw outside the line."

—**Atti Riazi**, CIO at United Nations

"Russell Sarder's passion for learning is genuine, contagious, and oozes off every page of *Building an Innovative Learning Organization.* This manifesto of ideas and recommendations on how leaders can, and must, build learning organizations is the right book for the right time. I am confident the book will change millions of lives for the better by inspiring countless numbers of chief executive officers to embrace learning as a primary corporate value and engage young people through learning programs predicated on meaningful internships, apprenticeships, and mentorships. Winston Churchill once said, 'Empires of the future will be empires of the mind.' *Building an Innovative Learning Organization* is the road map on how to build those empires."

> —**Gary J. Beach**, Publisher Emeritus of CIO Magazine
> and author of *The U. S. Technology Skills Gap*

"Russell Sarder is an innovative and ambitious businessman, as well as a voracious and inquisitive learner. Given his commitment to business and scholarship, it's a pleasure to see that he's dedicated a book to some of his most meaningful findings. Enjoy his insights, as this compilation is a derivative of hundreds of conversations with deep thinkers and exhilarating doers."

> —**Daniel Leidl**, PhD, Coauthor of *Team Turnarounds*

"Russell brings to life that one thing business has forgotten— learning. Learning is the core of every project, every business plan, every enterprise. The problem with our world is that we tend to see innovation as a big bang thing, a giant flash. In reality, innovation is like water on a rock, a steady, diligent process of perfecting that nurtures authentic products, bringing real value to customers and companies. It is like that famous story of the meeting of Alexander the Great and the Indian ascetic. One sees glory and success as a destination, the other as merely a journey."

> —**Hindol Sengupta**, Author of *Recasting India:*
> *How Entrepreneurship Is Revolutionizing the World's*
> *Largest Democracy* and Editor-at-Large of *Fortune India*

"Russell delivers sage advice and insight, cultivated by years of practical experience and engagement with many of the most influential business people of our time. The book is a gem."

—**David Hershfield**, Chief Product Officer at Auctionata

"Russell Sarder's *Building an Innovative Learning Organization* is a seminal treatise on the importance of organizational learning written by a world-class entrepreneur. In order to succeed, it's not enough to have basic compliance-driven training initiatives. The culture of learning must suffuse every part of the organization, from the mailroom to the executive suite. Russell eloquently makes the case that learning has the capacity to flatten management hierarchies, encourage collaboration, and help people identify mistakes. An organization that promotes learning is setting itself up for success in a competitive world. Russell's love of learning and intellectual curiosity permeates every page of this brilliant book."

—**Kabir Sehgal**, *New York Times* bestselling author of *Coined: The Rich Life of Money and How its History Shapes Us*

"Russell Sarder's latest book taps into the most basic human instinct—our ability to learn and adapt—and has intersected that instinct with the technologies of our modern age. Today's organizations' most existential threat is to be made redundant by disruptive technologies. *Building an Innovative Learning Organization* is the fulcrum that empowers organizations to harness the power of today's learning technologies against that threat. If you move a cannon by an inch, it changes the trajectory of the cannonball by a mile. If you read Russell Sarder's latest book, it will forever change the trajectory of your organization. Read it, be changed and more than survive—thrive!

—**Vincent Suppa**, Founder of HR Avant-Garde and Adjunct Professor at NYU

"The world is facing unprecedented challenges and megatrends— global demographic and global power shifts, urbanization, climate change, resource constraints, and new levels of transparency and disruption to business models driven by new, ubiquitous technologies and data. Only the most flexible organizations will make the shifts necessary to make their companies more resilient and help the world meet new challenges. Russell Sarder's *Building an Innovative Learning Organization* will help companies prepare for a new, volatile future by teaching them why it's so important to change, making a strong case for putting learning at the heart of an organization, and giving leaders frameworks and tools to get them there."

—**Andrew Winston**, Author of *Big Pivot*, *Green to Gold*, and *Green Recovery*

"How can your company thrive in the midst of rapid change? In *Building an Innovative Learning Organization*, Russell Sarder explains why we must expect and embrace change, and why lifelong learning is the key to continued success. He provides an essential framework for both job seekers hoping to work for the best companies in the world, and for executives who must stay ahead of the curve in a global, borderless business environment. This book will enable you and your organization to capitalize on emerging trends and develop an ongoing learning plan that drives your competitive advantage.

—**Dorie Clark**, author of *Stand Out and Reinventing You* and adjunct professor at Duke University, Fuqua School of Business

"Russell's commitment to advancing his enterprises is eclipsed only by his deep and passionate desire to see people and organizations better themselves through meaningful learning. Building upon his first book, Russell does a tremendous job of identifying a well-grounded framework for organizations and individuals. My hat is off to the man once again as he continues to push all of us to think, learn, and grow in new ways."

—**Russ Edelman**, CEO at Corridor Company, Inc. and Coauthor of *Nice Guys Can Get the Corner Office*

"Long before he became known as the 'CEO of Learning' and the host of Sarder TV, Russell Sarder was a well-known entrepreneur and the charismatic CEO of his own training company, NetCom Learning, where I taught many Project Management and Train-The-Trainer courses. Working with Russell, I was immediately impressed by his intellectual curiosity, and his keen interest in listening to others to learn what makes them succeed. I think these are key qualities that make him so effective in his interview series for Sarder TV, where he excels at bringing out the best in his interview subjects. I'm sure that the concepts, tips, and quotes captured from his Sarder TV interviews will help training managers improve the learning environments for their people, with the result of improving the efficiencies and profitability of their companies."

—**Jeff Furman**, Author of
The Project Management Answer Book

"Russell Sarder's love of learning is a contagious energy that gets into the bones of anyone who encounters him. Sarder TV was built on the principles of the new economy . . . the *Love Economy*. Sarder's approach of trade and reciprocity is as ancient as it is new. Today learning isn't optional. No longer will we find professionals who have not taken a course or read a nonfiction book since college. Russell Sarder sees the Internet and video as a way to share stories and some of the key learnings of thought leaders from all walks of business, the best practices that have built empires. Rather than reinventing the wheel, Sarder's book gives you fuel to fire up your life and your profession."

—**Karin Bellantoni**, President at BluePrint SMS

BUILDING AN
INNOVATIVE
LEARNING
ORGANIZATION

BUILDING AN

INNOVATIVE

LEARNING ORGANIZATION

A FRAMEWORK TO BUILD A **SMARTER WORKFORCE**,
ADAPT TO CHANGE, AND **DRIVE GROWTH**

RUSSELL SARDER

WILEY

Library of Congress Cataloging-in-Publication Data:

Names: Sarder, Russell, 1973- author.
Title: Building an innovative learning organization : a framework to build a
   smarter workforce, adapt to change, and drive growth / Russell Sarder.
Description: Hoboken, New Jersey : John Wiley & Sons, Inc., [2016] | Includes
   bibliographical references and index.
Identifiers: LCCN 2015036835 | LCCN 2015048173 (ebook) | ISBN 978-1-119-15745-8 (cloth);
ISBN 978-1-119-15746-5 (ePDF); ISBN 978-1-119-15747-2 (ePub)
Subjects: LCSH: Organizational learning. | Organizational change.
Classification: LCC HD58.82 .S27 2016 | LCC HD58.82 (ebook) | DDC 658.3/124–dc23 LC record
available at
http://lccn.loc.gov/2015036835

For my parents,
who raised me to become a passionate lifelong learner.

Contents

Preface

Anyone who stops learning is old, whether at twenty or eighty.[1]
—Henry Ford

When people discover that I launched NetCom Learning at the ripe old age of 21, they often ask, "Russell, how did a computer scientist from Bangladesh end up starting a business? How did a guy without any business experience become CEO of a successful company?"

"For one reason," I respond. "My love of learning."

My passion for learning is the dominant force in my life. My parents raised me to be curious, to read, and to ask questions, and in the process they helped instill in me a deep understanding that learning is the key to a successful, satisfying life. It is this passion for learning that took me from a middle-class boyhood in Bangladesh to my success as a leading American CEO.

Today I see that without realizing it, I built a framework for learning that has helped me focus on what I need to know and allows me to keep growing and developing new skills. I set learning goals and identified the competencies I needed, and then determined the best methods for mastering those competencies. I surrounded myself with mentors and hired coaches;

took courses in sales, marketing, communication, accounting and finance, leadership and management, and more; and read everything I could get my hands on. I applied everything I learned, using my business as a laboratory to test new skills and concepts.

As I developed more and more knowledge and expertise, I discovered that I could apply my personal learning framework to my business. By developing and implementing a learning plan that encompasses all levels of the organization, we have become a learning organization that is able to respond quickly to change and distinguish itself from the competition.

I believe that learning is the key to success for everyone and that everyone is capable of continuing to learn and grow throughout their lives. Dr. Edward Hess says it clearly in the title of his book: *Learn or Die.* The book is about learning organizations, but the statement is true for everyone, everywhere. Lifelong learning offers us the solutions to so many of the world's problems. Learning lifts people out of poverty, as evidenced by the success of effective learning programs for disadvantaged populations in developing countries and inner-city communities. Learning is the means by which we will find a way to save our environment before it's too late. Learning from our mistakes is how we keep from making those same mistakes again and again.

What Successful People Have in Common

There are a number of things that are important to success. Intellectual curiosity is important. People who are motivated and want to do well. But people who are self aware and understand their strengths and their weaknesses and work to improve themselves, who put people around them who help them play to their strengths and compensate for their weaknesses, make a big difference. Learning is a huge part of success. I say this to every young professional who is beginning a first job. More important than anything is learning.[2]

—*Hank Paulson*

The people we seek to emulate—people like Steve Jobs, Bill Gates, Bill Clinton, Oprah Winfrey, and Mahatma Gandhi—have certain characteristics in common: They are passionate about what they believe in, they work hard and stay focused on their goals, they are confident and competitive—and they are all lifelong learners.

But learning is not only vital for success in life and business; learning also makes us mentally stronger. When we learn, the connections between our brain cells grow stronger, and new pathways are etched into our brains. As Dr. Frances Jensen, a neuroscientist and author with Amy Ellis Nutt of *The Teenage Brain: A Neuroscientist's Survival Guide to Raising Adolescents and Young Adults*, told NPR's Terry Gross in 2015, "The whole process of learning and memory is thought to be a process of building stronger connections between your brain cells. Your brain cells create new networks when you learn new tasks and new skills and new memories. Where brain cells connect are called synapses. And the synapse actually gets strengthened the more you use it."[3]

What Successful Organizations Have in Common

If you are not learning, you're not moving forward and you can't be competitive. You can't even see what's coming towards you. For instance, what good is it if you're building the best buggy whip for a horse and buggy when cars are the disruptive innovation that's on the landscape? If you truly are committed to leading your organization and taking it to the next level, you have to always be making sure you're not building the best buggy whip.[4]

—Roseanna DeMaria

Successful organizations, such as Google, General Electric, the U.S. military, and Columbia University, also have certain characteristics in common: a flexible business model, a strong leadership team, sufficient resources, a clear understanding of their market segment, a clear focus on what drives profitability, and a clear understanding of their purpose—why the organization exists. They share another vital characteristic as well: They are learning organizations, able to remain competitive and continue growing in a rapidly changing global environment. They value, promote, and support learning at all levels and have learning plans and systems that enable them to translate that learning into action.

Learning organizations are better able to compete because they are more able to innovate and respond quickly to change in a world where change is one of the few things we can count on. The leaders of those organizations know that they can't move forward by standing still, and they can't pull ahead of the pack by doing things the same old way, year after year. Not satisfied with the status quo, they are constantly seeking ways to improve their products and services and differentiate themselves from the competition.

One reason that learning organizations gain the advantage is that they can attract, retain, engage, and motivate the best employees. Even during the recent recession, when many thousands of people were looking for work, organizations found it difficult to recruit good employees—and that is still the case. Learning organizations recognize that few people come equipped with all the necessary skills; instead, they seek employees who are willing and able to learn, have open minds, and are unafraid of change. Learning organizations also understand that today's best and brightest want more from their jobs than the security of a paycheck. Instead, they constantly seek opportunities to grow and develop their abilities.

About This Book

In this book, I share the framework that has helped both my organization and me succeed. You'll discover:

- Why learning organizations have the advantage in our rapidly globalizing, highly technological world; the key changes that affect an organization's ability to succeed; the characteristics of a learning organization; and a framework to guide your journey toward becoming a learning organization (Chapter 1)

- The importance of an organizational culture that values and supports learning at every level, how to recognize a learning culture, and what it takes to build a culture that attracts the best employees and helps the organization to continually improve (Chapter 2)

- How a learning plan helps you make your vision of a learning organization a reality, the components of a learning plan that serves as the foundation for your organization's transformation, and how to develop an effective learning plan that ensures your learning programs and activities are aligned throughout the organization (Chapter 3)

- The importance of developing learning goals at all levels of the organization, from senior executives to entry-level staff; how to create a goals cascade that aligns organizational, team, and individual learning goals with the organization's values, mission, and strategic goals; and questions to ask when setting learning goals (Chapter 4)

- What competency models are and how they serve as the foundation for recruiting, planning learning programs, and more; the four primary types of competencies an organization needs; the ways in which competency models are changing to address the needs of twenty-first-century organizations; and how to develop competency models for your organization and use them to assess learning needs (Chapter 5)

- An overview of the different ways in which people learn, the value of informal as well as formal learning, the five primary learning methods for helping people strengthen competencies and develop new competencies, criteria for selecting the best learning methods to meet individual and organizational goals, and ways to help ensure that people are able to apply what they learn (Chapter 6)

- The crucial role of ongoing evaluation to the success of your organization's learning plan, an overview of evaluation methodologies, how to develop measurement criteria, and questions for selecting the right evaluation methods (Chapter 7)

- How a comprehensive system for managing your learning operation helps ensure that your learning plans and programs remain aligned with your mission, vision, and business needs; how such a system keeps everything running smoothly and lets you respond quickly to change; the components of an effective learning operation; the roles of a CLO and a learning management service; and how to select the right learning technologies from a dizzying array of options (Chapter 8)

- Why the ability to succeed and thrive depends increasingly on not what people know, but how well they are able to learn;

what you can do to promote learning in your organization, in your community, and throughout the world; and how to become a lifelong learner yourself (Chapter 9)

About the Sarder Learning Framework

This book is not a scientific tome or an academic treatise. My learning framework, which has been tried and tested in my own company and with many of my clients, is based on real-world experience and knowledge gleaned from a vast array of sources, including:

- Respected authors, such as Peter Senge, Michael Marquardt, and Edward Hess
- CEOs and CLOs from Fortune 500 companies
- More than 50,000 NetCom Learning clients, who come from a vast range of organizations, including AOL, Coca-Cola, United Healthcare, Comcast, and the Walt Disney company
- Our NetCom Learning partners, who include Microsoft, Oracle, Autodesk, and Adobe Systems
- Learning professionals, including the more than 1,000 learning professionals who have taught classes for us over the past 17 years

Learning from Others

My constant search for opportunities to learn from others led me to start Sarder TV, an online media company that provides exclusive interviews with more than 150 leaders, authors, and learning professionals who share their insights about the ways in which learning is key to success. Because I believe so strongly in the power of learning from others, I have included excerpts from many of those interviews in this book. My hope is that sharing what others have learned will help you build a stronger organization, one that is able to succeed in the world of today *and* tomorrow.

—Russell Sarder, October 2015

1

Why Become a Learning Organization?

With tougher competition, technology advances, and shifting customer preferences, it's more crucial than ever that companies become **learning organizations**. In a learning organization, employees continually create, acquire, and transfer knowledge—helping their company adapt to the unpredictable faster than rivals can.[1]

— *David Garvin*

We constantly hear about the success of Google, which has topped *Fortune*'s best companies list for the past five years, where job applicants beat down the door to get in. We may not know as much about the other companies on the magazine's Best

100 list, such as Allianz Life Insurance Company, SAS, Edward Jones, and Children's Healthcare of Atlanta. What we do know is that, like any successful organization, for-profit or nonprofit, corporate or private sector, those organizations have this in common: They understand the value of learning.

The fact is that organizations don't succeed by staying the same. The landscape is littered with companies like once hugely successful Blockbuster. When Blockbuster filed for Chapter 11 bankruptcy in September of 2010, the prevailing theory was that it had been put out of business by Netflix or was a victim of the recession. In reality, Blockbuster put itself out of business. It went under because it failed to keep up with the changes in technology that gave customers options for the way they accessed film entertainment. Decision makers said, "Blockbuster is never going to go out of business. The Internet is too weak, too slow. There's not enough bandwidth." Yet, in the same difficult economy, Netflix thrived. The reason? As technology and customer preferences changed, Netflix looked ahead and was able to adapt.

Those lessons are everywhere. In *Good to Great to Gone: The 60 Year Rise and Fall of Circuit City*, Alan Wurtzel, son of Circuit City founder Sam Wurtzel, describes the collapse of one of the first and most successful big-box stores. At its peak, Circuit City had more than 700 stores and annual sales of $12 billion. But facing growing competition from upstarts such as Best Buy, Circuit City's management stubbornly held on to the business practices that had made it successful, unable or unwilling to change its business model to meet its customers' changing needs.

It's happening today. Amazon.com and Google hope to disrupt the package delivery business with drones that can drop packages right on your doorstep, bypassing UPS and FedEx. The *Wall Street Journal* quoted a UPS representative who said,

"There remain numerous reasons why drones are not a feasible delivery method at this time."[2] No one denies that drone technology isn't there yet and regulations still need to be put in place. But it seems more than possible that those obstacles will be overcome sooner rather than later, and when that happens, today's package-shipping companies could very well find themselves going the way of Blockbuster.

It could happen to us all.

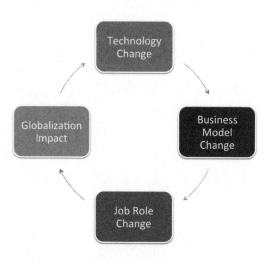

Key Changes That Affect Success.

Change comes in various forms. Our business models and strategies, which may have worked just fine for years, may no longer keep us relevant in the face of a global economy and changing customer preferences. We can no longer count on a stable, malleable workforce, because today's workers are quick to change jobs in search of new opportunities. Technology is changing so rapidly that we almost have to run in place to keep up, and we must keep up to stay ahead.

Changes in Technology

Information technology and business are becoming inextricably interwoven. I don't think anybody can talk meaningfully about one without . . . talking about the other.[3]

— Bill Gates

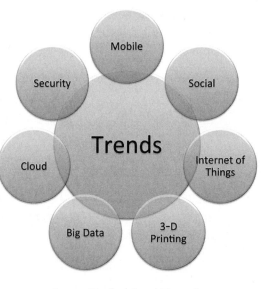

Seven Technology Trends

In a recent survey, GlobalWebIndex found that adults now spend close to two hours a day on social media.[4] Google processes more than 1 billion search queries every day. Every minute, more than 100 hours of footage are uploaded to YouTube—that's more content in a single day than all three major U.S. networks broadcast in the last five years combined. Facebook transmits the photos, messages, and stories of more than 49 billion people, almost half of the Internet population and a fifth of humanity. The *Wall Street Journal* projects that 28 billion devices—ranging from wearable devices to vehicles—may be connected to the Internet by 2020.[5]

Technology is changing the way we live, the way we work, the way we communicate, the way we get our information, and the products and services we want and need. We can compete only by anticipating and keeping up with the technology and leveraging it to drive our businesses. Today, that means understanding the potential impacts of seven technology trends: mobile, social, the Internet of Things, 3-D printing, big data, the cloud, and security.

Mobile. The hundreds of thousands of people in Times Square on New Year's Eve 20 years ago were using cameras with film to snap their photos of the big event. Now they all hold smartphones and send their photos across the world in a few seconds. My nephew in Bangladesh, a developing country, uses Skype on his phone to call me for advice about girls he meets on Facebook, which he also accesses on his smartphone. Apple recently released the Apple Watch, freeing customers of the need to reach into their pockets every time they want to make a call, check their e-mail, or do any number of other tasks. Tablet computers make it possible to write, read, and edit documents anywhere, at any time, without the need to lug around a laptop. All these mobile devices are having an earthshaking impact on the way we live, work, and do business.

Social. Survey after survey suggests that we spend a significant percentage of our waking time on social media. Think about what will happen a few years down the road when just about everyone has a smartphone, a smart watch, or some mobile device that hasn't even been invented yet. Everyone will be connected with everyone else, in all corners of the world. What will that mean for the way we do business? The way we run our workplaces?

The Internet of Things. Several of my friends use a wearable fitness tracker called Fitbit. You might even wear one yourself.

Almost 11 million of them were sold in 2014 alone.[6] Fitbit is part of what's called the Internet of Things, which essentially means anything that is connected to the Internet, which will increasingly include almost everything we use, from appliances to cars to medical devices. Brendan O'Brien, the chief evangelist and cofounder of Aria Systems, said, "If you think that the Internet has changed your life, think again. The IoT is about to change it all over again!"[7]

3-D Printing.   Perhaps the most potentially disruptive new technology is the 3-D printer. Straight out of *Star Trek*, the 3-D printer now lets you print just about anything, from a pencil holder for your desk to a replacement kidney, and the technology is only getting better. Researchers are even working on ways to print food products, electronic components, and more.[8] The *Wall Street Journal* predicts that this new *thing* is likely to disrupt our entire manufacturing industry.

Big Data.   According to the SAS Institute, "Big data is a popular term used to describe the exponential growth and availability of data, both structured and unstructured."[9] At the 2003 Techonomy conference, then Google CEO Eric Schmidt said that "every two days now we create as much information as we did from the dawn of civilization."[10] *Every two days!* That's an almost inconceivable amount of information, with crucial implications. Yet it's not the amount of information that is important. What's important is how we use it. We need people and technologies able to access it, store it, find it, analyze it, and determine how to apply it. The organizations that do that best will have a real competitive advantage.

The Cloud.   In an e-mail to employees on his first day as CEO, Microsoft's Satya Nadella said, "I believe over the next decade computing will become even more ubiquitous and intelligence will become ambient. . . . This will be made possible by an ever-growing network of connected devices, incredible computing capacity from the cloud, insights from big data, and intelligence from machine learning."[11] Nadella saw the trends: billions of mobile phones, the Internet of Things, and big data. All that information needs to be stored somewhere. That somewhere is *the cloud*, which implies a mist-like structure in the stratosphere but is simply another term for the Internet. Instead of filling up the hard drives of our computers, we now have the means of storing our files and data where we can access them from anywhere and share them with others when we wish. The cloud has both opportunities and challenges. We need a good understanding of the opportunities and challenges of this new technology so that we can use it to our advantage and keep our organizations running efficiently.

Security. Our increasing reliance on technology raises an increasing concern with security, and for good reason. As we move more and more of our data into the cloud, as we connect all our devices, from smartphones to refrigerators, to the Internet, as we spend an increasing amount of time on social media, we need to find ways to keep sensitive, confidential, and proprietary data out of the hands of hackers—and our competitors. How are we going to protect ourselves? What technologies and access policies do we need? These are questions we can't ignore.

Business Model Change

> Upscale grocery store chain Whole Foods (often referred to as "Whole Paycheck" because of its high prices) announced this week that it's launching a new offshoot brand—with lower prices—to appeal to younger, millennial shoppers.[12]
>
> — *Sam Sanders*

At Microsoft's Build 2015 conference, the company announced new Microsoft Azure data services for intelligent applications; Visual Studio and .NET tools and runtimes for Windows, Mac, and Linux; and APIs that enable developers to build rich applications with Office 365.

According to CEO Satya Nadella, "Microsoft has bold ambitions for platforms that empower developers across Windows, Azure and Office. Together, we will create more personal and more intelligent experiences that empower billions of people to achieve more."[13]

You can't move forward by standing still while things are changing all around you. Blockbuster and Circuit City went under because they failed to change their business models to keep up with a changing environment. In contrast, Microsoft, Whole Foods Market, and other successful organizations succeed because their business models and business strategies are works in progress that they modify constantly to stay abreast of—ahead of—changes in customer needs and preferences.

That's what we do at NetCom Learning. We opened our doors in 1998 as a provider of live, in-person technology and business training courses in various classrooms in the United States. As the technology evolved, we saw that the way our customers preferred to learn changed, too, which led us to reduce our focus on public, instructor-led, location-based courses and shift our emphasis to personalized, online blended learning— anywhere, anytime learning that our customers could access from any of their devices, from anywhere in the world. When we saw that an increasing number of organizations were starting to expand their learning and development programs, we shifted our business model again so that we could provide the advice and expertise they needed.

Job Role Change

Microsoft used to be a software company. Now it is building software for mobile devices and building its own devices.[14] Its software developers need to be able to develop applications for mobile devices instead of PCs. The company's leadership team needs to understand new technologies so that they can shift the company in the right direction. The marketing team needs to be able to reposition the company brand and use social media to market Microsoft's products. The sales team needs to be able to shift to the cloud version of the software from the original prepaid, licensed model.

When technology and business models change, certain jobs no longer become necessary, and new jobs need to be created, posing both challenges and opportunities for an organization and its employees. The organizations and individuals who are able to anticipate and prepare for these changing jobs have the advantage.

Globalization Impact

> Globalization has changed us into a company that searches the world, not just to sell or to source, but to find intellectual capital—the world's best talents and greatest ideas.[15]
>
> —*Jack Welch*

We live in a global world. Goods, people, ideas, and money move readily across borders. Events that happen on the other side of the world can quickly ripple through our own economy. Competitors are everywhere. New markets constantly emerge, and our customers are increasingly diverse. Our employees come from different cultures, and they have different experiences, expectations, and perspectives. All this interconnectedness has opened up vast new opportunities—and it presents many, many challenges. To gain the advantage, we need to understand what globalization means to us and learn to navigate its tricky waters.

The Learning Advantage

In this rapidly changing, highly competitive environment, learning organizations have a crucial advantage. They can respond more quickly and effectively to change. They are better able to keep ahead of the competition by coming up with innovative products and services. They are less likely to become mired in inefficient practices, more able to address problems quickly, and better at operating efficiently. Crucially, they are far more likely to attract and retain the best employees.

The Hiring and Retention Advantage

> When an employee feels listened to or invested in, they feel much more loyal to the organization because they feel that somebody cares about them.[16]
>
> *— Rachel Tuller*

Competing successfully in the war for talent can make the difference between an organization that continues to succeed, year after year, and one that withers away and dies. A few years ago, I asked a group of CEOs at the Inc. 5000 Conference, "What is the biggest challenge you are facing in your organization right now?" Almost 90 percent of them gave the same answer: "We are unable to locate the right candidate with the right skills at the right time." The respondents to a 2009 American Society for Training & Development (ASTD) Skills Gap poll agreed: 79 percent of companies surveyed reported that they faced skills gaps within their organization.[17] Yet, at the time the country faced a 10 percent unemployment rate. Only two years later, 3 million jobs were waiting to be filled,[18] and 65 percent of CIOs were struggling to locate skilled IT professionals.[19]

Although the economy has finally improved and the unemployment rate is (thankfully) dropping, large numbers of people are still looking for work. Yet organizations are still finding it difficult to recruit and retain the right employees.

Why is that so?

It's a complicated question, and there is no right answer. The impacts of globalization, changing technology, and changes in workforce demographics certainly contribute to the situation. Two other key factors are the shift to the knowledge economy and changes in the jobs themselves. People today seek jobs for which they are fully prepared but which no longer exist, while organizations try to find employees who come to the job "fully formed," with all the necessary knowledge and skills to jump right in on Day One.

Learning organizations have the advantage when it comes to hiring the best employees and keeping them from leaving in search of more attractive opportunities. That's because, given the choice, people want to work for organizations that give them the chance to develop and grow. A 2014 survey, *Global Human Capital Trends 2014*, by Deloitte, found that a primary reason employees leave their jobs is lack of opportunity. The same survey found that investments in training, development, and job mobility led to higher performance in organizations of all types.[20]

The Innovation Advantage

Becoming a learning organization will not only help your organization recruit the right employees but will also give your organization an advantage by making your employees better at everything they do. By not being locked into rigid hierarchies, stifled by bureaucratic procedures, and held back by outdated ways of thinking, you'll be able to bring the right people together at the right time to address problems and come up with innovative solutions more quickly than your traditional counterparts. As a learning organization, you won't sit at the side of the road like a car with a flat tire while your competition whizzes by. Instead, you will be constantly coming up with better products and services, better ways to meet customers' changing needs and preferences, and more cost-effective ways to meet your goals.

Investing in Learning Is Good Business

> Training and developing employees is much more than an employee benefit. It is a critical business driver that leads to high-performing employees and solid workforce retention.[21]
>
> — *GE Capital report*

According to Josh Bersin, writing in *Forbes*, American companies spent 15 percent more on corporate training in 2013—$70 billion in the United States and more than $130 billion worldwide, this after two previous years of increase.[22] That's no small change. But that investment can reap real, quantifiable rewards. That's why top organizations such as GE consider investments in learning and development as essential as those in research and development, marketing, and technology. Of the 12 industrials that formed the original Dow Jones Index, GE is the only one that remains part of that index. The company's success is attributed to legendary leader Jack Welch, who transformed it into a learning organization during his 20-year tenure as chair and

Learning Is . . .	
Opportunity	Empowering
Enriching	Survival
Confidence	Fundamental
Fun!	

CEO. During that period, GE's value increased by 4,000 percent.[23]

What Learning Is

> Learning: the activity or process of gaining knowledge or skill by studying, practicing, being taught, or experiencing something.[24]
> — *Merriam-Webster's Online*

Much of the learning that takes place in organizations is formal learning intended to meet a specific, immediate need, such as teaching someone to do a new task, improving team functioning, or preparing employees to take a certification test. That kind of learning is training: generally short term, practical, and focused on helping people do something or do something better.

Education, another type of formal learning, differs from training in that it is generally long term, not so focused on immediate needs. Education gives us the knowledge base that is the foundation for learning. It helps us understand concepts and continue developing our abilities. The impacts of education might not be apparent for a while, and they may never be obvious at all, but they are essential nevertheless.

Learning is not limited to formal programs with specific objectives. We learn constantly from what we read, from what we see in videos and on television, in our interactions with others, and from our daily experiences. Much of that learning goes unnoticed: You might come up with the answer to a question in conversation without realizing that you learned that information from something you read weeks or even months ago. You might find that you've become a better presenter, unaware that you'd picked up tips from watching a colleague at work. The leaders of learning organizations recognize the value of this kind of informal learning. They encourage people to learn from their everyday experiences and interactions in the course of their work.

What a Learning Organization Is

[A learning organization is a place where] people continually expand their capacity to create the results they truly desire, where new and expansive patterns of thinking are nurtured, where collective aspiration is set free, and where people are continually learning to see the whole together.[25]

— *Peter Senge*

A learning organization differentiates itself by valuing and supporting organization-wide learning from the top down. Learning is more than a menu of classes and online programs that employees can participate in when they need to close a performance gap. Instead, it is embedded in every aspect of the organization—in the ways in which decisions are made, problems are addressed, information is shared, the organization is structured, and the physical space is organized.

In a learning organization, the leaders continuously demonstrate by their words and actions their belief that learning is crucial to the organization's growth and ability to compete. The leaders are learners themselves who know that no matter how successful they are, and how much knowledge, experience, and expertise they possess, they always have a great deal more to learn. They know that learning comes from everywhere, so they elicit ideas and opinions from everywhere—from employees at all levels, as well as from customers, vendors, colleagues, competitors and others.

The leaders of a learning organization continuously strive to communicate their vision and promote the value of ongoing learning. But they do far more than just talk. They actively demonstrate that they care about employees' learning and development by providing the necessary resources. They share information openly and involve employees in the decisions that affect their work and their lives. They flatten hierarchies and eliminate unnecessary policies and rules. They encourage questions and reflection and create an environment in which people can easily collaborate and take risks. They help people to learn from their mistakes and see problems as opportunities.

A Framework for Building a Learning Organization

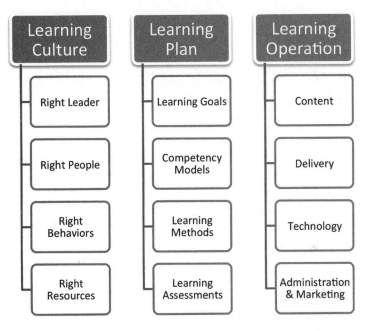

Sarder Framework: Building the Learning Organization

Building a learning organization doesn't happen just because you and your senior leaders think it's a good idea, and it doesn't happen overnight. It takes a long-term commitment, a deep well of patience, thoughtful planning, and a steady supply of resources. You'll need to build a learning culture, develop learning plans, and create a system for managing your learning operations. You'll find details about each of those key steps in later chapters. Here is an overview.

Learning Culture

The Components of a Learning Culture

Culture can be defined as "the sum total of ways of living built up by a group of human beings and transmitted from one generation to another."[26] It's culture that makes one country, region, or group of people different from another. It's easy to see those cultural differences when you travel, in such things as the food people eat, the way they behave, the way they dress, and their celebrations and rituals.

Organizations also have unique cultures that shape their workplaces, and it's that culture that differentiates a learning organization. In contrast with traditional hierarchical organizations, the culture of a learning organization promotes and supports learning at all levels and in a variety of ways.

To build a learning organization, you must deliberately and consciously transform the existing culture into a learning culture. Accomplishing that transformation requires the right leaders, the right people, the right behaviors, and the right resources.

The Right Leader

> Setting the example is all about . . . *putting* your money where your mouth is. It's about *practicing* what you preach. It's about *following through* on commitments. It's about *keeping* promises. It's about *walking* the talk. It's about *doing* what you say.[27]
> —*Jim Kouzes and Barry Posner*

Transforming an organization's culture starts at the top. The CEO and leadership team must have the vision and the will. They must *want* to build a learning culture. They must *believe in* the value of learning. Most of all, they must *be learners* themselves. Leaders who are passionate learners communicate their vision and continuously promote the value of learning throughout the organization. They help people understand why learning is important to achieving both the organization's goals and their own. But they do more: They walk the talk. They set the example by being learners themselves. They create and maintain a learning environment, provide learning programs and activities, and reward learning efforts.

The Right People. You can't build a learning organization alone. A learning culture is built by its people. To transform your organization's culture, you need people who have open minds, are good collaborators, are willing to question the status quo, are not afraid of change, and welcome opportunities to learn. Learning organizations actively seek such people among their current employees and when they recruit and hire.

The Right Behaviors. Collaboration, innovation, experimentation, risk taking, and information sharing are hallmarks of a learning organization. In such organizations, people challenge established ways of doing things and explore new ideas for getting better. People are actively engaged in the learning process and openly share their learning with others.

You may encounter resistance when you try to encourage these behaviors. We human beings seem to be naturally designed to resist change. Most of us find it easier to keep doing things the old way, no matter how ineffective or cumbersome, than to step out into the unknown and take the risks involved in trying something new. Harvard business professor Rosabeth Moss Kanter cites three causes of this resistance to change: loss of control, uncertainty, and surprise.[28]

That resistance to change is one reason why you need to involve people at all levels—even people outside of the organization, such as key clients, consultants, and vendors—in building a learning organization. Involving people helps reduce their resistance by giving them some control over what is to be changed, reducing the uncertainty about what might happen as a result, and eliminating the surprise that comes when decisions are made opaquely and at the top. There's another benefit as well: You may find that some of the best ideas about how to go about the process come from your line staff, not from your managers.

The Right Resources. Traditional organizations often consider learning and development as something to be supported only when the resources are available and something to cut back when they are not. But treating learning as a discretionary expense not only makes it difficult to maintain a vibrant learning and development program throughout the organization but also sends a clear message that the organization doesn't consider learning all that important.

The leaders of learning organizations recognize that learning is an essential cost, and they demonstrate their support by providing the necessary resources, even when times are tough. Following the Sarder Principle, they spend at least 2 percent of their total revenue on learning and development.

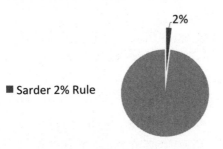

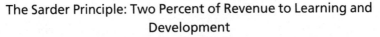

■ Sarder 2% Rule

The Sarder Principle: Two Percent of Revenue to Learning and Development

Learning Plan

The Components of a Learning Plan

Your learning plan describes what will be done to translate your vision of a learning organization into reality. It includes organizational, team, and individual learning goals; the competencies needed to achieve goals; the learning methods you will use; and the ways in which you will evaluate outcomes.

Learning Goals.   The goals in your learning plan provide targets to aim for by describing what you hope to accomplish within specified time frames. They also help ensure that your learning initiatives clearly align with the organization's mission, values, and strategic goals.

Your learning plan will have three levels of goals: the organization's learning goals, learning goals for each team, and individual learning goals for each employee.

Learning Goals Cascade

Organizational learning goals describe the desired outcomes of learning initiatives that help the organization achieve its strategic goals. Team learning goals describe what the team will do to get better at helping the organization achieve its mission. Individual learning goals describe what individual employees will learn to get better at their jobs and advance their careers. Goals at every level help keep everyone focused and heading in the same direction.

Learning goals are particularly important for individuals because well-thought-out goals can increase people's motivation to learn. Children do not need that motivation—they learn because they are naturally curious about the world, and some carry that curiosity into adulthood. But once we become adults, most of us need a specific reason to embark on a learning process. We'll learn for personal reasons: taking classes in art for our own enjoyment, studying computer programming or getting an MBA to improve our job prospects, or reading histories or fiction because we like to see the world through other people's eyes.

At work, however, people often see learning as unnecessary and irrelevant, a waste of their time (and too often it is). They will sit through a class or do the exercises in a self-study program, but their attention is elsewhere. As a result, they are unlikely to remember or apply what they've learned.

In a learning organization, people know *why* they are learning. Learning programs and activities are clearly linked to organization, team, and individual success. People participate actively in developing their own learning plan, so they have some control over their learning and understand its importance. They are held responsible for their own learning, and they are rewarded for learning efforts and success.

Competency Models. For your organization to succeed, you need people with the knowledge and ability to do certain things. Competency models describe what your employees need to know and be able to do for the organization to achieve its strategic goals. Job descriptions are based on competencies, and your recruiting efforts focus on the competencies required for a specific job. But even the most qualified and experienced employees have gaps between the competencies they need and the ones they have, and employees may need new competencies when things change. Your learning plans address the gaps between the competencies your organization needs and the ones your employees have.

Learning Methods. Your learning plan describes the learning methods you will use to help people close specific competency gaps: classes, e-learning and Web-based programs, coaching, mentoring, and on-the-job training.

When selecting learning methods, it's important to understand that learning is not a one-size-fits-all activity. As educators know, some children learn well by sitting silently at their desks listening to the teacher or reading, while others need to see pictures or demonstrations and still others learn best when they are active.

It's the same with adults. Some learn best by listening, others by watching, and others by doing. Some prefer to work in groups, while some do better working on their own. Learning programs that fail to consider these differences may not meet everyone's needs, so when designing or purchasing programs, you need to consider how effective they will be for different types of learners. Your choice of learning methods will also be affected by what people need to learn, the urgency, where learners are located, the time they have available for learning, your budget, and more. The more you know about the options, the better able you will be to select the right learning methods for a given situation.

Learning Assessments.   Organizations make a significant investment of time, effort, and money to develop and implement their learning strategies. Unfortunately, many neglect to take the steps needed to determine how well—even whether—their investment is paying off. Even the most costly and most well attended learning programs may be doing the organization and its employees little good. Programs that were useful when they were first implemented may go on and on like the Energizer Bunny, well past the point at which they have ceased to be relevant.

Successful learning organizations build a variety of assessment measures into their learning plans so that they can constantly track and evaluate their learning programs. They collect, share, and analyze data about how well programs are meeting both organizational and individual needs, and they reevaluate programs that are not working as intended, are no longer relevant, or are no longer necessary.

Learning Operation

The Components of a Learning Operation

If you've ever been involved in building or remodeling a house, you know that there are seemingly innumerable tasks and numbers of people involved. Without someone to organize, plan, oversee, manage, and direct the project, the expensive endeavor is likely to degenerate into a shambles.

In the same way, there are lots of tasks and people needed to plan, develop, organize, implement, and evaluate organizational learning. To achieve their goals and use resources efficiently, top learning organizations centralize learning operations under a single contractor, so to speak, an individual, team, or outside professional who makes sure that everything gets done, and done smoothly; data and information are readily accessible; tasks and activities are coordinated; and unnecessary redundancy is avoided. A carefully managed learning operation that covers content, delivery, technology, and administration and marketing facilitates access to learning, keeps learning programs and materials current, and provides tools for identifying needs and measuring outcomes.

Content.   Carrying out learning initiatives involves a huge amount of content: learning programs and materials, competency models, performance and needs assessments, evaluations, instructor and vendor information, and more. You will need to develop or purchase a system for collecting all that content, organizing it, keeping it up to date, and ensuring it can be easily accessed when it is needed.

Delivery.   Today's organizations have many options for delivering learning, and it's not always easy to decide which ones will be the most effective and cost-efficient Managing your learning operations includes choosing the right option or options to fit your budget, meet specific goals, and match both learner and organizational needs.

Technology.   Technological tools are essential for managing twenty-first-century learning operations. But it's amazingly easy for organizations to spend huge sums of money on technology and still be unable to manage their learning initiatives effectively and efficiently. It's vital to understand the options so you can select those that are right for you.

Administration and Marketing.   A staggering number of tasks are involved in managing learning operations, from storing and organizing assessments and materials to purchasing, developing, updating, and scheduling courses to letting people know what's available to overseeing tuition reimbursement programs to negotiating with vendors. Whether you handle these tasks in-house or outsource them to a company that specializes in managing learning operations, a centralized administrative and marketing function helps you control costs and ensure that everything gets done and done right.

To Consider: What are some ways in which becoming a learning organization can benefit your organization?

What's Next: Building a learning organization means transforming the culture so that learning is valued and supported at every level. That's what we'll discuss in Chapter 2.

Building a Learning Culture

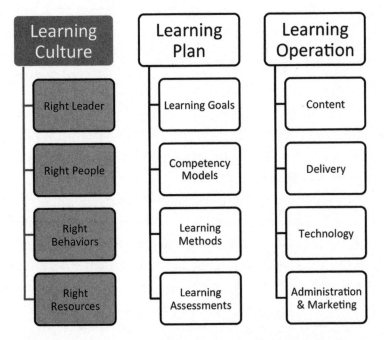

Sarder Framework: Building the Learning Organization

Just as nations have distinct cultures, organizations have distinct ways of believing, thinking, and acting that are manifested by the symbols, heroes, rituals, ideology, and values. The nature of learning and the manner in which it occurs are determined in large measure by organizational culture.[1]

—*Michael Marquardt*

Imagine you are a consultant who has been brought in to observe two organizations, both of which are about the same size and in similar industries. Following are some of the things you notice:

Organization 1. The open space is broken up into a maze of cubicles that wall people off from one another. Managers have private offices around the periphery of the space, and the larger the office, the higher up the manager. Employees often have to knock or make an appointment to gain access. Employees seldom see the executives and senior managers, who are on a floor of their own, with a private dining room. Access to senior managers is only by appointment. When you ask people, "How does the work you do contribute to the organization's success?" most of them shrug, or say, "How should I know?" The meetings you observe are run by managers or team leaders, who do most of the talking. Training is offered haphazardly, and although there is a tuition reimbursement program, few employees take advantage of it. There is a high rate of turnover.

Organization 2. Employees and managers alike work in large open spaces around central conversation areas set up with low tables and comfortable chairs. Conference rooms scattered around the space and conference rooms around the periphery are available for people to use when they need them. Some senior managers have private offices, but their doors are usually open; employees are encouraged to drop in at any time. Managers are more likely to be seen meeting or talking with employees than sitting in their offices. Everyone seems to know the CEO and senior managers, who can often be seen talking with individual employees or small groups in a conversation space or the cafeteria. Every employee you speak with is able to describe the way his or her work contributes to the organization's success. Meetings are led by team members, not by managers and team leaders; they are lively and fast paced, with lots of questions, information sharing, debates, and active participation from everyone. The organization has a chief learning officer who is responsible for a wide range of learning initiatives, including in-house and online courses, mentorships, and a robust tuition reimbursement program, and participation in programs is very high. Recruiters attract large numbers of applicants, and people tend to stay in their jobs for a long time.

You probably recognize Organization 1. You may have worked in a similar company—it might even resemble your own. It's a traditional hierarchical organization in which people are expected to do what they are told to do in the way they are told to do it, without questioning its value or the way it is done. In these organizations, learning has value only when it is seen as essential to job performance. People tend to resist change and hoard information. Serious mistakes may be kept secret unless something happens to bring them out in the open. We see the results in companies such as Enron and, more recently, General Motors.

Organization 2 may be less familiar, although the description is beginning to fit an increasing number of workplaces. This organization has a culture for the twenty-first century, where organizations must be prepared for rapid change and intense competition. In these organizations, employees are actively encouraged to question the status quo and to share information and ideas freely. Instead of resistance to change, the prevailing attitude is "Let's keep getting better!" Learning is a priority for everyone, from the top on down, and mistakes are seen as an essential part of learning as people ask, "Why did that happen?" and "What can I (or we) do to improve?" The success of organizations such as Google, SAS, and even the U.S. Army points to the effectiveness of this culture in today's rapidly changing, rapidly paced environment.

How to Recognize a Learning Culture

[People] greet with kisses on the cheek. Elders are respected by kissing their right hand, then placing the forehead onto the hand. . . . The concept of sharing a bill is alien. . . . Best is to graciously thank the host then later invite them to a restaurant [and] inform the manager not to accept payment from them.[2]

—A guide to Turkish customs

When you first visit a new country or region, you become aware of the ways in which the culture differs from your own. You may notice that people hug or kiss one another on each cheek when they meet or that they greet one another by shaking hands or bowing. They may eat their main meal at midday or in the evening. They may dress formally, in casual clothes, or in regional garb. Women, men, and children eat together or they eat separately. They take off their shoes when they enter a home, or they do not. They laugh and talk loudly in public, or they are more reserved. They ask strangers personal questions and share personal information, or they talk only about politics and the weather until they know one another better.

Travel guides offer basic knowledge about key aspects of national or regional cultures, so you can learn ahead of time about the expected behavior in a particular country or region. But the culture of an organization is rarely described in writing. Instead, it is made visible by such things as the physical layout of the space;

the policies, procedures, and rules; the words people use and the means they use to communicate with one another; how people dress and what they put on the walls; the stories they tell; and the events and celebrations they hold. In other words, you know it when you see it.

New employees learn "how things are done around here" mostly by osmosis. Even though they may not be able to articulate easily what they've learned, it doesn't take long before they discover what behavior is okay and what is not, what and what not to say, and what is valued and what is not.

Organizational cultures don't just spring into being. They evolve over time, usually reflecting the personalities and values of their founders or initial leaders, with unconscious or deliberate alterations by subsequent leaders. That's what happens when you transform a traditional organization into a learning organization: You alter its culture.

How to Build a Learning Culture

The Components of a Learning Culture

Culture is what people do when no one is looking.[3]

—*Herb Kelleher*

Conscious shifts in attitudes, beliefs, and behavior happen only over time and with constant effort. Peter Senge, author of *The Fifth Discipline* and one of the world's preeminent thinkers on leadership and management, explains that "it is a testament to our naïveté about culture that we think we can change it by simply declaring new values." But, Senge continues, "deep beliefs and assumptions can change as experience changes, and when this happens, culture changes."[4]

Transforming your organization's culture requires a long-term commitment to action from you and the organization's senior leaders. You may remember from Chapter 1 that a learning culture has the right leaders, the right people, the right behaviors, and the right resources. Those four essentials are the foundation of your learning organization. They each play a vital role in a learning culture.

The Right Leader

Leader: a person who rules, guides, or inspires others.[5]

Leaders come in many forms. Autocratic leaders, such as Stalin, Muammar al-Gaddafi, and Kim Jong-un, rule by fear: People follow them because they have no choice. But throughout history, great leaders, such as Abraham Lincoln, Nelson Mandela, Martin Luther King Jr., Mahatma Gandhi, the Dalai Lama, Cesar Chavez, Angela Merkel, and Aung San Suu Kyi, have inspired followers by conveying a powerful vision, setting the tone, and serving as role models for others to emulate.

The leaders of successful organizations, whether they are for-profit or nonprofit, public or private, or large or small, do the same. Their visions inspire people, and through their actions, they serve as role models that other people seek to emulate. In their years of research, Jim Kouzes and Barry Posner, authors of *The Leadership Challenge*, one of the best-selling leadership books of all time, found that "among admired leaders, one quality stands out . . . commitment to a clear set of values and [passion] about their causes."[6]

Learning organizations have leaders with a vision of what they want the organization to be, a commitment to and a passion for learning, and a belief that learning is vital to the organization's growth, ability to compete, and ability to achieve its goals. Those leaders set the tone and engender trust. As Kouzes and Posner say, they set a positive example and "mobilize others to want to get extraordinary things done." To carry out their vision, they create a safe, supportive environment in which people are encouraged to speak their minds, hear and respect opposing ideas, take risks, and learn from mistakes.

Begin with the Vision

> A vision gives employees and the entire organization an overarching goal that helps guide strategic thinking and planning . . . people are more inclined to accomplish tasks that serve a purpose they understand and embrace. . . . Vision generates powerful, creative learning [and] provides a focus that keeps learning processes and efforts on course in the face of stress, frustration, and impatience.[7]
>
> *—Michael Marquardt*

> Every organization, every social movement, begins with a dream. The dream or vision is the force that invents the future. . . . Leaders gaze across the horizon of time, imagining the attractive opportunities that are in store when they and their constituents arrive at a distant destination. . . . Their clear image of the future pulls them forward.[8]
>
> *—James Kouzes and Barry Posner*

In 2001, when former CEO Doug Conant began his tenure at the Campbell Soup Company, the company was in dire straits. Its stock was falling, and it had fallen well behind its competition. The new CEO knew that his job would not be easy. But he had a vision of what he wanted the organization to be, and with careful planning and lots of hard work, he was able to lead Campbell employees to turn the flailing company around. Eight years later, Campbell was outperforming the Standard & Poor's 500, the employees were highly engaged, and the company was considered one of the most socially responsible of all U.S. companies.[9] That success began with Doug Conant's vision.

Share the Vision

> When everyone [in the organization] has the same goal, the new organizational [learning] vision will enjoy unparalleled enthusiasm and support. . . . [Vision] generates powerful, creative learning that leads to high-quality products and services. It also provides a focus that keeps learning processes and efforts on course in the face of stress, frustration, and impatience.[10]
>
> —*Michael Marquadt*

Making a change of any kind begins with the desire to change and the vision of what change looks like. Building a learning culture in your own organization starts with your vision of what you want the organization to be. But for your vision to become reality, you need to share it.

Be a champion of learning. Seek opportunities to promote learning as a value. Communicate openly and frequently about what a learning organization is and why you believe that learning is vital to the organization's success. Bring up learning in conversations and get people talking about what it means to be a learning organization. Incorporate learning in discussions of everyday business matters and in your memos, presentations, and newsletters. As you talk about learning, clearly link it to the organization's mission, values, and business goals. Convey your expectation that learning should be part of everyone's job, at all levels of the organization. Help people see how opportunities for learning exist in every activity.

Be a Role Model

> Titles are granted, but it's your behavior that wins you respect. . . . Exemplary leaders know that if they want to gain commitment and achieve the highest standards, they must be models of the behavior they expect of others. *Leaders model the way.*[11]
>
> —*James Kouzes and Barry Posner*

Your responsibility as a leader is to set the example. If you truly believe in building a learning culture, show by your actions and words that you consider learning a high priority. Be a learner yourself, and share what you learn with others. Follow through on your commitments and promises. Be open to new ideas and different points of view. Admit your mistakes and demonstrate the ways in which you use mistakes as learning opportunities. Ask for help when you need it. Let others know that you believe you have a lot to learn from them, and encourage them to share information, feedback, advice, suggestions, and opinions. In conversations and meetings, ask open-ended questions and listen attentively to the responses. Use positive language: Instead of saying, "Yes, but . . ." try saying, "Yes, and. . . ." That response, which conveys respect for people's opinions and ideas, encourages the openness and collaboration that is essential to a learning culture.

The Right People

A learning organization needs employees who have the right motivation for and approach to learning—a learning mindset. . . . [They] hire and develop people who like to learn and who proactively seek to learn.[12]

—*Edward D. Hess*

An organization's ability to succeed depends on its employees, and the leaders of a learning organization value their employees as their most important asset. The transformation to a learning culture means recruiting the right employees. Successful learning organizations recognize that it's not enough to hire people who are skilled engineers, computer programmers, marketers, or salespeople. Instead of focusing only on people whose qualifications perfectly match the job, they look for people who are also active learners, who are always looking for ways to do a better job, and who seek opportunities to learn something new. People with those characteristics are more open to new ideas and more willing to share information with others. Change doesn't frighten them. They welcome challenges and see mistakes, difficult tasks, and problems as learning opportunities. Those are the people who will be good at collaboration and who care that what they are doing matters.

The Right Behaviors

In most traditional workplaces, employees are reluctant to speak out when they think something is wrong or could be done a better way. They feel safer and more comfortable doing things in the same old way, even if it's not working well. Chances are that they are discouraged from acknowledging mistakes or challenging decisions made by higher-ups. The prevailing attitude is "Keep your head down and do your job, and you'll be fine."

Learning organizations are very different. People are constantly talking to one another, sharing information and knowledge, and debating ideas. They may argue about the right way to do something, but they respect one another even when they do not agree. They try new things, and when they fail, reflect on the reasons so they can do better the next time.

Those behaviors are risky. As Kouzes and Posner write in *The Leadership Challenge*, "People never do anything perfectly the first time they try it—not in sports, not in games, not in school, and most certainly not in work organizations. When they engage in something new and different, people make a lot of mistakes. That's what experimentation is all about, and, as research scientists know very well, there's a lot of trial and error involved in testing new concepts, new methods, and new practices . . . [and mistakes] are part of the price people pay for innovation and for learning."[13]

Learning is hard work. People are likely to be thrown off balance as they struggle to understand a concept or master a skill, and they are understandably reluctant to try new things if they're afraid they'll look foolish—or worse, be punished—when they stumble and make mistakes. To enable the right behaviors, you need to create a safe environment that supports learning behaviors—an environment in which employees at all levels feel safe speaking out and taking the initiative, in which they know that their ideas and suggestions, even their criticism, are valued and will be taken seriously, and in which mistakes are seen as an integral part of learning to do a better job.

To build a learning culture, enlist all your managers in conveying the vision and creating a supportive environment that is conducive to learning. Managers at every level should set the example by being learners themselves, acknowledging their own mistakes, sharing information, and eliciting employees' ideas. Establish the expectation that a key part of a manager's job is to help employees learn. Help them see themselves not as bosses who need to maintain control but as coaches and facilitators who help people perform at the highest level. Ensure they make time for employees to learn, share what they have learned with others, and use their learning on the job; hold people responsible for their own learning; and reward both efforts and successes. Encourage them to include learning in casual conversations and discuss how learning helps both them and the organization achieve their goals. Make sure they let employees know that they consider mistakes an essential part of the learning process and see problems as opportunities for change.

To create a learning environment, streamline policies, procedures, rules, regulations, and structures that may obstruct the open exchange of information, collaboration, and innovation. In many organizations, ideas for change must receive approvals at several levels. Information is shared only on a need-to-know basis. Teams operate in relative isolation, and crossing over is discouraged. Cumbersome, outdated procedures create unnecessary redundancy and discourage change, so eliminate unnecessary rules, regulations, and layers of approvals. Reduce hierarchies. Minimize the boundaries between departments and work units.

A Note of Caution. Changing a bureaucratic organizational structure takes time, and those kinds of changes can make people uncomfortable until they get used to the new ways of doing things. Be sure to involve employees and managers at all levels in determining what changes need to be made and how to make them.

Organize your physical spaces to encourage communication and collaboration. Dan Hoffman, former CEO, president, and general manager of M5 Networks, Inc. of ShoreTel, says it well: "I believe that your physical space needs to reflect the culture absolutely. Having an open space encourages communication, collaboration, candor and transparency."[14] Hoffman knows that the configuration of the physical work environment has a significant impact on the ways in which people communicate and interact with one another. Walls keep people apart, so if you want to encourage frequent, open communication, take down the walls that separate people from one another. Create spaces in which people can run into one another during the course of the day, and set up comfortable, open seating areas in which they can have informal conversations. Bring managers and executives out from behind closed doors and private dining rooms so that they become part of the everyday conversation.

The Right Resources

Many organizations pay lip service to the idea of learning. They agree it's important, something they need and should encourage. So why isn't every organization a learning organization? One reason is that learning initiatives and programs can be costly. As we discussed in Chapter 1, many organizations see learning and development as discretionary, so they are among the first items to be cut when operating budgets need to be trimmed.

Learning organizations such as GE have a distinctly different point of view. They know that valuing learning is not enough. Instead, they believe that learning and development (L&D) are so vital to their success that they include it on their line-item budget, year after year.

For your vision of a learning organization to be more than a good intention, you need to commit the necessary resources to cover both direct and indirect costs on an ongoing basis. Direct costs are those associated with designing, purchasing, administering, monitoring, and assessing courses; hiring consultants and instructors; travel, equipment, space, and materials; and the technology for delivering and managing learning operations. Depending on the size and complexity of your organization, you may want to create a manager of L&D or chief learning officer position to manage and oversee the planning and implementation of learning initiatives, or you may choose to contract with an outside company that can handle those responsibilities. You may incur costs for reconfiguring your physical space and reimbursing employees' tuition.

You also need to consider indirect resources that do not show up as line items in your L&D budget. The most important of those resources is your employees' time. People need time away from their work so that they can take courses and participate in learning activities, and they need extra time when they first begin applying new concepts and techniques to their work; they may also need time to travel to the site of a learning program. It may take more time for a group of people to collaborate than for one person simply to decide how to solve a problem. Managers need to spend time working with employees to identify learning needs, help them develop learning plans, and support their learning efforts.

Learn How You Are Doing

Building a learning culture requires finding out what you are already doing well and what you need to change. What attributes of a learning organization does your organization currently have? Do you need a full-scale makeover? What changes will you need to make in leadership, people, behaviors, and resources to become the learning organization you envision?

To determine what changes you'll need to make, do a comprehensive assessment. Use questionnaires, surveys, and focus groups to gather information from people at all levels of the organization, from line staff to senior management, as well as from customers, vendors, and others. All those differing perspectives help to create a valid, accurate picture of the current situation.

For your assessment to be useful, leave enough time, and provide the necessary resources. If your staff has the necessary expertise and the right tools, you can conduct the assessment in-house. Otherwise, you can use an off-the-shelf instrument, such as the online *Learning Organization Survey*, published by professors David A. Gavin, Amy C. Edmondson, and Francesca Gino, or bring in experienced professionals.

How Are We Doing? These kinds of questions can help you assess the extent to which your organization already has the characteristics of a learning organization and identify what you may need to change.

Do we continuously ask ourselves what's working, what's not, and what we can do to get better?

☐ Yes, to a   ☐ Seldom,   ☐ To some   ☐ Don't
   great extent   if ever   degree   know

Do our managers and leaders acknowledge mistakes and ask for help when they need it?

☐ Yes, to a   ☐ Seldom,   ☐ To some   ☐ Don't
   great extent   if ever   degree   know

(continued)

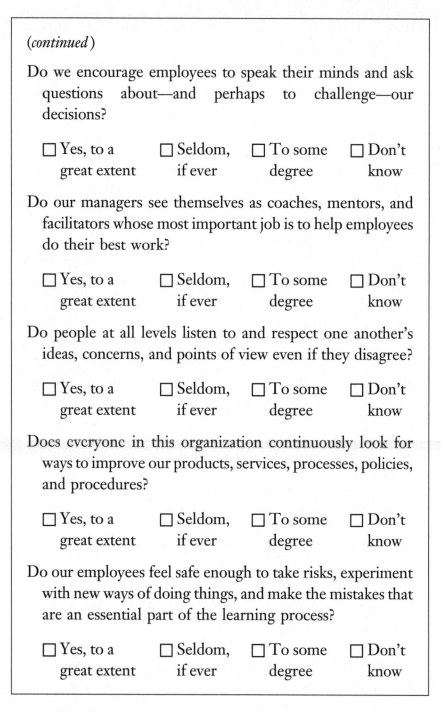

(continued)

Do we encourage employees to speak their minds and ask questions about—and perhaps to challenge—our decisions?

☐ Yes, to a   ☐ Seldom,   ☐ To some   ☐ Don't
    great extent   if ever   degree   know

Do our managers see themselves as coaches, mentors, and facilitators whose most important job is to help employees do their best work?

☐ Yes, to a   ☐ Seldom,   ☐ To some   ☐ Don't
    great extent   if ever   degree   know

Do people at all levels listen to and respect one another's ideas, concerns, and points of view even if they disagree?

☐ Yes, to a   ☐ Seldom,   ☐ To some   ☐ Don't
    great extent   if ever   degree   know

Does everyone in this organization continuously look for ways to improve our products, services, processes, policies, and procedures?

☐ Yes, to a   ☐ Seldom,   ☐ To some   ☐ Don't
    great extent   if ever   degree   know

Do our employees feel safe enough to take risks, experiment with new ways of doing things, and make the mistakes that are an essential part of the learning process?

☐ Yes, to a   ☐ Seldom,   ☐ To some   ☐ Don't
    great extent   if ever   degree   know

Do managers, teams, and individuals at all levels openly share information and have ready access to the information they need?

☐ Yes, to a   ☐ Seldom,   ☐ To some   ☐ Don't
   great extent   if ever   degree   know

Have we eliminated policies, procedures, and structures that create unnecessary bureaucracy?

☐ Yes, to a   ☐ Seldom,   ☐ To some   ☐ Don't
   great extent   if ever   degree   know

Do we value learning enough to include learning and development as an essential budget item even when times are tough?

☐ Yes, to a   ☐ Seldom,   ☐ To some   ☐ Don't
   great extent   if ever   degree   know

Are our employees engaged in their work?

☐ Yes, to a   ☐ Seldom,   ☐ To some   ☐ Don't
   great extent   if ever   degree   know

Do people seek ways to help one another succeed?

☐ Yes, to a   ☐ Seldom,   ☐ To some   ☐ Don't
   great extent   if ever   degree   know

Are we able to attract and retain the employees we want?

☐ Yes, to a   ☐ Seldom,   ☐ To some   ☐ Don't
   great extent   if ever   degree   know

(continued)

(continued)

Do our human resources and compensation policies reward people for learning and for helping others learn?

☐ Yes, to a great extent   ☐ Seldom, if ever   ☐ To some degree   ☐ Don't know

Do managers give people the time they need to learn, reflect on their learning, and apply what they learn on the job?

☐ Yes, to a great extent   ☐ Seldom, if ever   ☐ To some degree   ☐ Don't know

Do we offer a variety of learning options to meet a diversity of learning needs and styles?

☐ Yes, to a great extent   ☐ Seldom, if ever   ☐ To some degree   ☐ Don't know

Do we ensure that learning goals, initiatives, programs, and activities are clearly aligned with our mission, values, strategic goals, and business needs?

☐ Yes, to a great extent   ☐ Seldom, if ever   ☐ To some degree   ☐ Don't know

Do our senior leaders serve as role models by being learners themselves?

☐ Yes, to a great extent   ☐ Seldom, if ever   ☐ To some degree   ☐ Don't know

Do our employees understand the value of learning to their own and the organization's success?

☐ Yes, to a great extent   ☐ Seldom, if ever   ☐ To some degree   ☐ Don't know

Do we use technology such as social media and electronic bulletin boards to help people learn and share what they learn?

☐ Yes, to a great extent   ☐ Seldom, if ever   ☐ To some degree   ☐ Don't know

Do we learn from and share our learning with our customers, vendors, and others outside the organization?

☐ Yes, to a great extent   ☐ Seldom, if ever   ☐ To some degree   ☐ Don't know

Do our senior managers seek input from others both inside and outside the organization before making important decisions and then clearly explain the reasons for those decisions?

☐ Yes, to a great extent   ☐ Seldom, if ever   ☐ To some degree   ☐ Don't know

Do we learn from other organizations' best practices?

☐ Yes, to a great extent   ☐ Seldom, if ever   ☐ To some degree   ☐ Don't know

(continued)

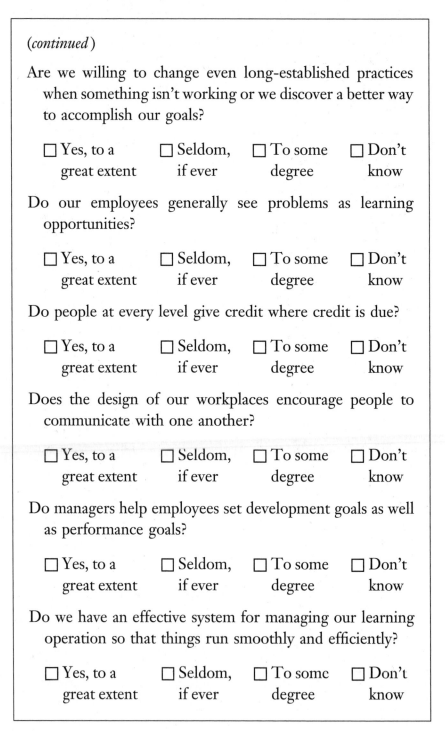

(*continued*)

Are we willing to change even long-established practices when something isn't working or we discover a better way to accomplish our goals?

☐ Yes, to a great extent   ☐ Seldom, if ever   ☐ To some degree   ☐ Don't know

Do our employees generally see problems as learning opportunities?

☐ Yes, to a great extent   ☐ Seldom, if ever   ☐ To some degree   ☐ Don't know

Do people at every level give credit where credit is due?

☐ Yes, to a great extent   ☐ Seldom, if ever   ☐ To some degree   ☐ Don't know

Does the design of our workplaces encourage people to communicate with one another?

☐ Yes, to a great extent   ☐ Seldom, if ever   ☐ To some degree   ☐ Don't know

Do managers help employees set development goals as well as performance goals?

☐ Yes, to a great extent   ☐ Seldom, if ever   ☐ To some degree   ☐ Don't know

Do we have an effective system for managing our learning operation so that things run smoothly and efficiently?

☐ Yes, to a great extent   ☐ Seldom, if ever   ☐ To some degree   ☐ Don't know

Do we assess our learning programs regularly to see how well they are working and make necessary changes?

☐ Yes, to a   ☐ Seldom,   ☐ To some   ☐ Don't
    great extent   if ever   degree   know

To Consider: How would you describe your organization's current culture? Is it more like Organization 1 or Organization 2? What are some of the changes that may be needed to transform it into a learning culture?

What's Next: Building a learning organization requires more than a vision and good intentions. It requires careful planning. In the next chapter, we'll examine how to develop the learning plan that serves as the foundation for your organization's transformation.

3

Developing a Learning Plan

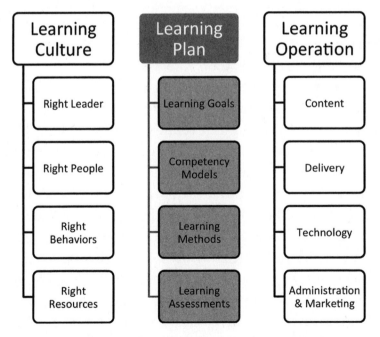

Sarder Framework: Building the Learning Organization

Always plan ahead. It wasn't raining when Noah built the ark.[1]

—*Richard Cushing*

Planning is bringing the future into the present so that you can do something about it now.[2]

—*Alan Lakein*

Change begins with an idea: a desire to make something happen, solve a problem, do something new, or become better. Implicit in the idea of change is a vague understanding of the desired outcome: "Let's improve the morale around here." "Let's provide more relevant services to our community." "Let's be more sustainable." "Let's become more profitable." "Let's become known as a great place to work."

Everyone has great ideas. But few of them become reality. That's because having an idea about what you want to accomplish is only the starting place. Actually accomplishing it takes a great deal of thought and lots of hard work. And it takes a plan. Without a concrete, carefully developed plan, even the best ideas and the most worthwhile dreams soon wither away.

That's what often happens to the idea of building a learning organization. The CEO comes back from a conference on competition in the twenty-first century filled with ideas. She calls her executive team together. "We have to shore up our training efforts. We need to get everyone learning!" HR is given new mandates. Managers are told to provide (unspecified) learning opportunities for their employees. An HR associate is assigned the responsibility for setting up a corporate university. Memos go out to all the employees, encouraging them to sign up for learning programs. Yet, by the end of the first year, the initial enthusiasm has waned. Some employees—who enjoy learning or need training for a specific purpose—may take a few courses, but the majority show little interest. The responsibility for learning and development remains isolated in an HR department with little decision-making authority and an unreliable budget. Limited resources are spent on flavor-of-the-month programs that are not targeted to meet specific organizational or individual needs.

For your vision of a learning organization to become reality instead of fading away in the face of what appear to be more urgent priorities, you need a comprehensive learning plan that includes an overall organizational learning plan, a learning plan for each team, and a learning plan for each employee. Like the itinerary for a trip, that plan will lay the foundation for your learning and development initiatives by clearly describing where you are going and how you will get there. By providing a learning infrastructure for the organization as a whole, your learning plan helps ensure that the efforts of everyone in the organization are directed at the same common goal: to make the organization better.

The Components of a Learning Plan

The Components of a Learning Plan

There are four essential components to a learning plan:

- **Learning goals,** which describe what you hope to achieve at the organizational, team, and individual levels

- **Competency models,** which describe what people in the organization need to know and be able to do to accomplish the organization's mission and strategic goals

- **Learning methods,** which describe the ways in which people will learn what they need to achieve the desired competencies

- **Learning assessments,** which measure the success of your learning plan

In the next four chapters, we explore each component in detail. Here's an overview.

Learning Goals

> Building a learning organization is a lot like building a house. A house needs a supporting foundation, electrical and plumbing systems, a roof, and an insulated structure. These components must be integrated and aligned to work together to produce the desired results.[3]
>
> —*Edward Hess*

You'd have to answer a lot of questions and make a lot of decisions before starting to build a house. What kind of house do you want——ranch style? Traditional? Modern? How many bedrooms and bathrooms do you need? Should it have one story or two? How many square feet? Do you want a fireplace? A swimming pool? A formal dining room? What's your budget? Your time frame?

For the house-building process to succeed, you need to clearly describe your goal—the situation that will exist when the house has been completed: "By March 1, 2016, we will have a 2,000-square-foot modern home on one level with three bedrooms and two and one-half baths, a full kitchen with eating area, a family room with fireplace . . . for a cost not to exceed. . . ." The goal describes the desired future state—the situation that will exist when the goal has been achieved. That's what all goals do, whether they are personal goals, family goals, community goals, business goals, or learning goals.

In top organizations, team and individual goals at every level are clearly linked to the organization's values, mission, and business needs. That linkage keeps everyone on the same page, so to speak, helping to align learning efforts, ensure the efficient use of resources, and increase employees' understanding of the importance and relevance of the work they do. (See Chapter 4 for more on developing learning goals.)

Competency Models

Competencies refer to the ability to use the specific set of related skills, knowledge, and abilities that are needed to carry out certain tasks or functions. Every organization needs people with specific competencies. To build that house, you need an architect who is able to design the home and develop the blueprints that will guide its construction; a contractor who is able to manage the construction process; and skilled craftspeople—carpenters, electricians, and many others—who are able to carry out specific construction tasks.

The competency models in your learning plan describe the competencies that people in your organization need for you to be able to achieve your mission and strategic goals. Let's say you've set a business goal of launching at least one new product every year for the next five years. To accomplish that goal, you need employees who are good at analyzing the market, innovating, collaborating, designing and building prototypes, testing, and more.

Once you've identified the essential competencies, you can identify the gaps between the competencies that people have and the ones you need. If an organizational goal is to use technology to increase the free flow of information, what technologies do people have already that they can use? What technologies do they need to learn how to use? (See Chapter 5 for more on competencies.)

Learning Methods

New York diners are famed for their huge menu options, from scrambled eggs and toast to matzo ball soup to hamburgers, chicken Kiev, and Boston cream pie, all available at any hour of the day or night. Fortunately, you won't have that many options when selecting the best learning methods to address a learning gap. But an understanding of your choices helps you select the method or combination of methods most likely to help people attain the desired competencies in the most cost-effective way.

Learning methods generally fall into five categories: physical or virtual classroom programs; self-study, such as reading, self-paced e-learning, and video or audio podcasts; on-the-job training; mentoring; and one-on-one coaching. In a well-functioning organization, peer-to-peer learning also takes place every day in informal discussions and work groups, knowledge is shared freely, and people are encouraged to seek out the learning in every situation.

The Five Primary Learning Methods

There is no best learning method. The choice depends on such wide-ranging factors as what is being taught, the urgency of enabling change, the learners' locations, and the available budget. An off-the-shelf, self-directed e-learning program might be the quickest, most cost-effective way to help people become proficient in new technology. On-the-job training could be the most practical way for someone to learn a new job. A mentor can be an invaluable source of information and advice for a person who wants to become a better leader. A well-designed classroom program might be the most effective way to help people become better at collaborating.

There's another important factor to consider when selecting learning methods: differing learning styles and preferences. Some people learn well on their own, and others prefer to learn in groups. Some learn better by reading than by listening, some by seeing visuals or demonstrations, and still others by doing. The most effective learning programs are designed to meet these differing needs. (See Chapter 6 for more on learning methods.)

Learning Assessments

There has been a great deal of controversy recently about student testing. School boards, educators, parents, and legislators are engaged in an ongoing and often heated debate about whether there are too many tests and whether students are learning anything besides how to perform on tests. The answers are probably "yes" and "yes." But what is often lost in the somewhat heated discussions is the primary purpose of testing: to find out how well educational programs are working and, if students are not achieving their learning goals, determine what changes need to be made.

The purpose of assessing your organization's learning programs is the same—to determine how well your learning plans are working and to determine what changes you need to make. Without ongoing assessment, programs may be continued long after they have ceased to be effective or relevant, with the result that resources are wasted and people see little reason to consider learning to be of any value.

Just as there are many different learning methods, there are different ways to assess the success of learning programs and activities, all of which seek to answer a number of important questions:

- Are we accomplishing what we set out to accomplish? How well are we achieving our goals? If we are not achieving our goals, why not?

- Has the internal or external situation changed since this learning plan was implemented? Are the goals still relevant? Still achievable?

- Are we using resources as efficiently as possible? Are there more cost-effective ways to help people close performance gaps? To help them continue to grow and develop?

- Are the results worth the effort and expense? What is the actual return on our investment?

Form a Team to Develop Your Learning Plan

Organizational learning plans don't spring into being overnight, and they don't result from a few hours of brainstorming at an executive retreat. They may take months or even years to develop. But it's worth taking the time and making the effort to do it right. Your learning plan serves as the foundation for your organization-wide learning efforts. A hastily conceived plan may end up torpedoing your efforts, leaving people feeling frustrated, confused, and reluctant to engage in the hard work of learning.

An effective learning plan is a collaborative effort, so start by forming the right team—people who can gather and assess information about your needs and challenges, identify goals and priorities, decide on learning methods, and determine how outcomes will be measured. A strong team will be diverse in terms of perspectives, knowledge, and areas of expertise. That means drawing team members from differing areas and levels of the organization and perhaps including customers and others from outside the organization as well. A diverse team is more likely to develop a plan that addresses real, relevant needs and challenges and aligns with your organization's mission, values, and business needs. Including a wide range of people also makes it easier to get organization-wide buy-in once the plan has been completed.

Consider Team Size and Composition

> Bigger is better—if you are a cellphone company. But if you are
> a project team, the opposite should be true.[4]
>
> —*Abhay Padgaonkar*

A cohesive, functional team should be large enough to provide sufficient diversity but small enough so people can readily communicate with one another and meet as a group as needed. Fewer than 5 to 7 members may be too small; more than 12 to 15 may be too large. Make sure every person counts—that there is a good reason to include each individual on this team.

Seek people who are open-minded, are flexible, and value learning. For team members to work well together and be committed to what is likely to be a complex, long-term project, they must be willing to consider other points of view, make changes in response to new information or changes in the situation, and believe that learning is important to success.

Hold a Kickoff Meeting

Bring team members together for at least one face-to-face or virtual meeting to lay the groundwork for the project. Use the meeting time to help them get to know one another, which will make it easier for them to work together. Explain why the organization has decided to develop a learning plan and what it hopes to accomplish. Connect learning to the organization's mission, values, purpose, strategies, and vision. Discuss the ways in which the learning plan that the team develops will be used and how it will benefit both the organization as a whole and the individual employees. Make sure that everyone is willing to make a commitment to a long-term project.

Use the kickoff meeting to establish specific project goals, identify what actions need to be taken to achieve them, and decide who will be responsible for what. Create a time line that includes checkpoints and deadlines.

Establish Communication and Reporting Protocols

Open, ongoing communication is essential to team functioning. Agree on what methods will be used to keep everyone informed of progress, issues, and changes. Establish a forum in which team members can ask questions of one another, share ideas and information, and voice any concerns that may come up as the project moves forward.

Arrange to Meet Regularly during the Life of the Project

Periodic meetings help team members remain connected to one another and to the project. Set up a meeting schedule, and ask team members to put all the meetings on their calendars. Agree that any team member may call a special meeting if it becomes necessary to discuss critical issues. If team members are in different locations, use a virtual meeting room so members can see one another and everyone can participate. Circulate an agenda ahead of time so everyone can come prepared.

Plan for Contingencies

One of the few certainties we have in this life is that things do not always go as planned. Explore "What if?" scenarios: What if team members drop out, necessary information is not available or not what you expected, or there are significant internal or external changes that affect the project?

Assess the Current Situation to Identify the Organization's Needs and Challenges

> Using quick-fix solutions to close performance gaps [that affect core business processes] can be harmful . . . A strategic needs assessment examines the internal and external factors that affect performance within the context of an organization's business strategy and identifies the gaps between the current and desired conditions.[5]
>
> —*Kavita Gupta, Catherine M. Sleezer, and Darlene F. Russ-Eft*

Your organizational learning plan will describe what you will do to effect change: the actions you will take to close the gap between your current state and your desired future state. So, what is it about the current state that needs to be changed? Why?

The answers to those questions lie in your business goals. Thus, the more useful question is "What do we need to do better to achieve our business goals?"

For example:

- "We need to do a better job of keeping up with rapid technological change."

- "We need to be able to attract and retain the best employees."

- "We need to be more competitive in the global marketplace."

- "We need to expand into new products, services, or markets."

- "We need to increase profitability by reducing waste and inefficiency."

- "We need to go green so we will be more responsible members of our community."

It's not enough to guess at what gaps need to be filled to achieve your desired future state. Successful learning plans are based on data that shows clearly where you are now and what you need to change. Only then can you determine which gaps can be addressed by learning and which must be addressed in other ways.

Collect the Data

To identify the organization's learning needs, you need information about the current situation—a great deal of information. You may already have some of it, but you will undoubtedly need more. This part of the process can require significant resources, including time, expertise, and money. But rushing data collection or failing to do a thorough job may mean that parts of your learning plan are based on incomplete or inaccurate information, leading to wasted time and resources down the line.

Collection methods, which can include metrics and statistics, questionnaires and surveys, focus groups, observation, interviews, and more, depend on the type of data: quantitative or qualitative.

Quantitative (*quanti*ty) data deals with numbers. It tells you *what* is going on by measuring how much, how many, how often, how well, and how fast. Quantitative data can be presented in visual form—charts, graphs, and tables—that make it easy to see changes over time and compare one thing to another.

Examples: Increases and decreases in sales, costs, and production time; number of employees who stay longer than . . . ; reductions in product defects; and increases and decreases in productivity.

Qualitative (*quali*ty) data deals with things that can be observed but not measured. It tells you *why* something is or is not happening and helps you understand *what* you can do differently to improve. Qualitative data is presented not in numbers but in words. Its purpose is to gain understanding: Why is this so? What do people think (or care) about . . . ? What do they want (or not want)?

Examples: What new products (or services) do customers want us to provide? Why are sales dropping? What motivates our employees to be more productive?

Use the Results of the Team's Assessment

> Throwing resources at problems or opportunities is like throwing a chocolate pie at the wall and hoping some of it will stick: the action is more likely to create a mess than an improvement; furthermore, it is a waste of good resources.[6]
> —*Kavita Gupta, Catherine M. Sleezer, and Darlene F. Russ-Eft*

> It is not an intelligent strategy to train people to overcome system deficiencies. Instead, we should design the system properly to make sure that the performers can leverage all their capabilities.[7]
>   —*Klaus Wittkuhn*

Let's back up a little. Remember that the purpose of collecting and analyzing data is to identify your organization's learning needs and develop a comprehensive plan for addressing them. But your research is likely to uncover a great many gaps between the current state and your ideal future state, and not all those gaps can be addressed by learning.

Organizations often rush headlong into training and development programs with the assumption that learning is the solution to a problem. In reality, many of the gaps between current and ideal future states result from organizational or systems problems or insufficient resources, information, equipment, tools, or technology. For example, learning won't help employees become better collaborators if the organization's policies limit the free flow of information. Learning programs will do little to improve customer service if you don't have enough representatives to keep up with customer calls.

Before blindly assuming that learning is the path to success, work with your team to answer these questions:

- What are the gaps between where we are now and where we are going? In other words, what do we need to do better to achieve our business goals?

- What are the reasons for those gaps? Can we improve the situation by changing any systems, processes, policies, or procedures? By restructuring? Changing our hiring or incentive practices? Providing resources, equipment, space, tools, or technology? What changes do we need to make before a learning plan can be effective?

- Which gaps can be addressed by helping employees at all levels learn new skills, gain new knowledge, or change their attitudes?

- Which of our learning needs and challenges are the most important to address? What is likely to happen if we don't address them?

- Who are the stakeholders? Who, both inside and outside the organization, is likely to be affected by, or involved in, addressing our learning needs and challenges?

- What issues, limitations, and constraints must we consider when developing and implementing our learning plans? Are there time pressures? Do we have or can we get the necessary funds? Are we likely to encounter resistance to change from managers? Employees? Are we subject to any legal requirements that mandate training on specific topics, such as safety or regulatory compliance?

Once you've answered those questions—and it can take a while—you will be ready to develop the learning goals that will provide the basis for your organization-wide, team, and individual learning plans. That's what we'll cover in the next chapter.

To Consider: What are some current challenges your organization faces? Which of them might be addressed by learning?

What's Next: Learning goals for employees at all levels of the organization, from senior executives to entry-level staff, are essential components of your learning plan. In Chapter 4, we'll look at how to develop useful, relevant, meaningful learning goals that help the organization and its employees succeed.

CHAPTER

4

Setting Learning Goals

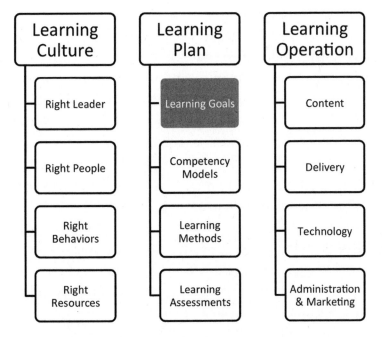

Learning Culture	Learning Plan	Learning Operation
Right Leader	Learning Goals	Content
Right People	Competency Models	Delivery
Right Behaviors	Learning Methods	Technology
Right Resources	Learning Assessments	Administration & Marketing

Sarder Framework: Building the Learning Organization

The organization that makes it a priority to develop quality, effective goals will succeed in its performance management, in its business . . . and in developing its employees' skills and confidence. . . . Goal setting, given high priority and approached consistently throughout the organization, is the mechanism by which the business delivers results.[1]

—*Oracle white paper*

In essence, a goal is a written statement that describes where we are headed, what we will do to get there, and the situation that will exist when we've arrived. In life and at work, goals keep us focused on what's important and keep us from wasting our valuable time doing things that will not help us get where we want to be. We've all set out to achieve personal goals at one time or another: to become proficient at a musical instrument, to play tennis or golf, to prepare for a marathon, to lose weight or stop smoking, or to transition to a better job. Goals are the mechanisms by which our intentions become reality.

An organization uses strategic goals to focus energy and resources on achieving its mission. Strategic goals describe specific actions the organization will take to succeed, such as increase sales, launch new products, become more profitable, or enter new markets—or become a learning organization. Well-functioning teams use goals to guide their efforts in helping the organization achieve its business goals. Individuals use goals to get better at their jobs and continue their growth.

In top-performing organizations, team and individual goals flow from the organization's overall goals, ensuring that everyone is headed in the same direction and activities align with the organization's mission, values, and overall strategies. This goal structure is often referred to as a *cascade*.

Learning Goals Cascade

Mapping goals in this way helps everyone in the organization see the relationship of the work he does to the organization's success. Clear, relevant goals clearly linked to the organization's mission, values, and strategic goals help employees know what is expected of them, which Gallup research has found measurably increases employee engagement.[2]

Linking goals at every level helps organizations use the resources they commit to learning as efficiently as possible. Unfortunately, that's not always what happens. Even when funds are tight, many organizations waste money and employees' time on learning initiatives, courses, and programs that fail to make any measurable difference. A training and development department working in relative isolation may create and purchase courses that people do not need or want. Managers push employees to participate in programs that have little relevance to their jobs or their career paths. Even when learning is relevant and important, people may be so busy with other priorities that they end up with little or no opportunity to apply what they learn.

That's why your organization's learning plan must include learning goals for the organization as a whole, for teams, and for employees at every level, from senior executives to newly hired line staff. Learning goals that flow from your strategic goals throughout the organization establish the context necessary to ensure that everyone understands what needs to be learned and why the learning is important.

All Goals Are Not Created Equal

There's a S.M.A.R.T. way to write management's goals and objectives.[3]

—*George T. Doran*

Useful learning goals are more than a simple statement describing an intention: "Improve my career prospects by becoming a better writer." "Become proficient at using PowerPoint to prepare presentations." "Spend more time with my family by using my work time more efficiently." Useful goals meet certain criteria. The most important is that they include *actions* that clearly state what the person will do to achieve the goal. If a manager's intention is to become better at delegating, the actions might include taking a self-study course and working with a coach. If a paralegal's intention is to become an attorney, the actions might include enrolling in an online program and taking weekend classes at a local law school.

But it's not enough simply to state what the person will do. Goals must also describe how success will be *measured*. They must contain within them the answer to the question, "What will the learner be able to do when she has achieved the goal?" Pass a certification exam? Write a report or analyze a financial statement? Fix a truck so that it passes an inspection? Deliver a presentation to the satisfaction of a designated observer?

Finally, a useful goal includes a *time frame* that describes a deadline or a period during which the person will take the actions for achieving it: "Within the next six months," "by the end of the current quarter," "whenever thus-and-so occurs during the next year." Without a time frame, the most relevant and important goal can get lost in the frenzy of day-to-day activities.

The acronym SMART is commonly used to describe a useful goal. Experts in the learning and development field define the letters in the acronym in various ways, but these definitions are common:

S = Specific: A SMART goal uses concrete verbs that clearly describe the actions that will be taken to achieve the desired change.

M = Measurable: A SMART goal describes actions that can be measured or evaluated in some way.

A = Attainable: A SMART goal is realistic. It describes something that can actually be accomplished, considering the situation and the available resources (including time).

R = Relevant: A SMART goal is meaningful. It describes something that is worth doing within the context of the situation.

T = Time based: A SMART goal states the time frame during which the actions will be taken or the results achieved.

The SMART acronym is a guideline, not a prescription. The focus should be on the action plan for achieving the goal and on ensuring that the goal is meaningful and relevant, so people can clearly see the value of spending time and effort to achieve it.

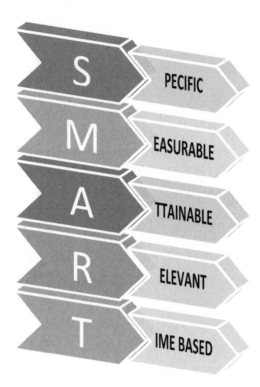

SMART Goals

When it comes to learning goals, there is another factor to consider. Useful learning goals are not only attainable but also challenging. Researchers have found that encouraging people to stretch themselves, to go beyond what they think they can do, increases their engagement. For example, psychologist and author Mihaly Csikszentmihalyi demonstrated that people are happiest when they are in a "flow state," so absorbed in an activity that nothing else seems to matter.[4] In *A Theory of Goal Setting & Task Performance*, Edwin Locke and Gary Latham cite Locke's research showing that specific and challenging goals led to better task performance than vague or easy goals.[5]

Learning Goals versus Performance Goals

> The primary distinction between performance and learning goals lies in the framing of the instruction. . . . A performance goal . . . frames the instructions so . . . [the] focus is on task performance (e.g., attain 20 percent market share); . . . a learning goal frames the instructions in terms of knowledge or skill acquisition (e.g., discover three effective strategies to increase market share).[6]
>
> *—Gary Latham and Gerard Seijts*

The performance evaluation process in most organizations is designed to give employees feedback that lets them know what they are doing well and what they need to improve to meet the requirements of their job. Those are performance goals, which focus primarily on the outcome: Assemble a piece of equipment without error, meet a sales target, convey an attitude of service to customers, or write reports that meet specific standards. Performance goals are written with the assumption that the person already has at least some of the necessary knowledge, skills, or abilities.

But performance goals are not always learning goals. In fact, some performance goals are achievable without much if any learning: An employee might be able to meet a sales target by being given access to better prospect lists; a customer service representative might become better at conveying an attitude of service by being allowed more time to spend with each caller.

A learning goal has as its focus something more than simply getting better at doing something. It helps people acquire the knowledge they need to increase their understanding and be able to apply what they learn. That's not to say employees do not need performance goals. They do. But having more of a focus on learning goals makes people more valuable by helping them increase their knowledge, skills, and abilities, not just helping them meet a performance target. Learning goals help people grow and expand. They encourage employees to think for themselves, find new ways of doing things, and feel more empowered at work.

Performance Goals versus Learning Goals

Performance Goal	Learning Goal
Win a tennis game against a player with similar skills	Improve your serve and return so you can win against a player with similar skills
Meet your project deadlines 95 percent of the time for the next six months	Meet project deadlines 95 percent of the time for the next six months by using your time more efficiently
Write proposals that get us 20 percent more invitations to meet with clients	Write proposals that clearly explain how we will address client needs as expressed in their requests for proposals

Development Goals

A learning goal may set a target for improving specific skills, knowledge, or abilities that an employee needs to meet or exceed the requirements of his current job. Development goals are learning goals that help people go beyond those requirements so that they can take advantage of new opportunities, move up in their careers, or even enter an entirely new field.

As we discussed in Chapter 1, top learning organizations understand the importance of employee development to their ability to attract and retain the best people. Today's employees are seldom content to sit back, meet job requirements, and collect a paycheck. A survey of top talent by Sylvia Ann Hewlett and Carolyn Buck Luce found that 90 percent of men and 82 percent of women who love their high-earning, 60-hours-a-week jobs do so because those jobs are challenging and stimulating.[7]

The message is clear: Employees today want new challenges, opportunities to stretch themselves, to explore new ideas, and to develop new skills.

In short, they want to learn.

How to Set Learning Goals

Useful learning goals are not developed in isolation. They result from collaboration among employees, their managers, and, perhaps, human resources representatives who examine the current situation, identify the gaps between the competencies the person has and what the person needs, determine what changes to make, and identify the specific actions to take. The process begins by asking the following kinds of questions.

What does the person want to learn? One reason that Google has been at the top of *Fortune*'s Best Places to Work list for four years running is that it encourages and supports employees' learning in a variety of ways, such as reimbursing them for up to $12,000 a year in tuition costs. The company makes that investment because it recognizes that for most of its employees, development goals are just as important as goals that address specific performance gaps. Your learning plan also needs to include development goals and ways to support and reward development efforts. Increasing employees' skills and knowledge makes them a more valuable asset, and providing development opportunities also helps you attract and retain forward-thinking, open-minded people who seek an organization in which they can learn and grow.

What issues, constraints, and limitations need to be considered when setting learning goals? One of the SMART criteria is "attainable." Unrealistic goals may sound good on paper, but in reality they are counterproductive. When people become frustrated because they are unable to achieve a learning goal despite their best efforts, they lose motivation and interest in the learning process. Goals may be unrealistic because they are too much of a stretch, the time frame is too short, there are too many conflicting priorities, or the learning opportunities are not available. A realistic learning plan sets goals that are attainable within the specific situation.

How will you know when—and whether—the goals have been achieved? When you fly to Paris, you know you've arrived when the pilot comes on the speaker to point out the Eiffel Tower below. A well-written goal contains its own Eiffel Tower, a description of the situation that will exist when the goal has been reached. A useful goal also includes a deadline and milestones for checking progress along the way. If you've set an organizational goal to streamline your policies and procedures within six months, you might set monthly milestones so you can keep the project on track and address any issues that come up.

To Consider: Does everyone in your organization, including those at the very top, have written goals? Are they SMART goals? How well do you think those goals align with the organization's mission, vision, values, and business goals? In what ways could shifting the focus from performance goals to learning goals help you build a learning organization?

What's Next: Competency models describe what people in your organization need to be able to do for the organization in order to achieve its mission and strategic goals. They serve as the foundation for recruiting, planning learning programs, and more. In the next chapter, you'll learn why competency models are important and how to develop them for your organization.

Creating Competency Models

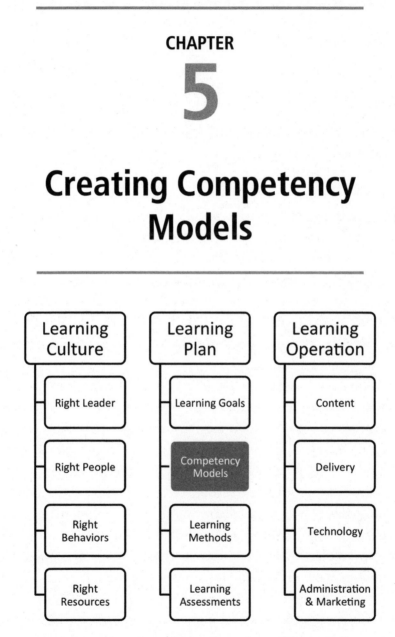

Learning Culture	Learning Plan	Learning Operation
Right Leader	Learning Goals	Content
Right People	Competency Models	Delivery
Right Behaviors	Learning Methods	Technology
Right Resources	Learning Assessments	Administration & Marketing

Sarder Framework: Building the Learning Organization

A competency model is a framework for organizing a collection of observable skills, behaviors, and attitudes that impact the quality of work that people do. It describes what people need to know and be able to do in order to execute on their responsibilities effectively.[1]

—*Melissa Noonan*

For every job . . . the No. 1 thing we look for is general cognitive ability, and it's not I.Q. It's learning ability. It's the ability to process on the fly. It's the ability to pull together disparate bits of information.[2]

—*Laszlo Bock*

Imagine a theater without people who can act or build sets; a hospital without people who can care for patients, handle admissions, and prepare meals; or a software company without people who can develop new products and sell them. Organizations accomplish their goals through the combined efforts of individuals. They can succeed only if they have individuals with the necessary *competencies*: the right knowledge, skills, abilities, attitudes, and attributes.

The idea of using competencies to predict success has been around for more than half a century. As early as 1959, psychologists observed that "without clear competency criteria, recruiters select, managers manage, trainers train, and career planners plan to different (and sometimes even conflicting) images of the capabilities required to do a job."[3] In 1973, Harvard University psychologist David McClelland found that competencies based on criteria established by an analysis of top performers were a better predictor of success than experience, academic credentials, or intelligence and aptitude tests when selecting Foreign Service Information Officers.[4] Subsequent research by McClelland and many others led to the development of *competency models*, which are carefully structured collections of the competencies an organization needs to achieve its strategic goals within the context of its vision, mission, and culture.

Competency models are frameworks that describe critical success factors: what people need to know and be able to do to accomplish a job at the highest level. Top-performing organizations use them in various ways, including:

- **Talent**—to recruit and select the right employees
- **Skill Gaps**—to identify employees' performance gaps and development needs and help them recognize the value of continuous learning
- **Learning Plan**—to develop learning plans (learning goals, competency models, learning methods, and learning assessments)
- **Performance**—to set performance and development standards and goals, and clarify job expectations
- **Productivity**—to maximize employee productivity
- **Change**—to drive organizational change
- **Purpose**—to help employees understand how their work contributes to the organization's success

Knowledge, Skills, and Attitudes (KSAs)

Competencies are essentially descriptions of what learning and development experts refer to as KSAs, the knowledge, skills, and attitudes (also referred to as abilities or attributes) that individuals need to be top performers in specific jobs.

Learning Domains (KSAs)

The acronym KSA has been used since the 1950s, when Dr. Benjamin Bloom and a group of colleagues at the University of Chicago identified three broad categories, or *domains*, that describe three types of learning:

Knowledge (cognitive domain): Refers to intellectual activity, such as acquiring, analyzing, evaluating, and applying information and concepts; awareness, information, or understanding of the facts, principles, rules, theories, or processes needed to perform a task.

- Write clear, informative, accurate research reports
- Diagnose problems with defective products
- Follow Equal Employment Opportunity Commission regulations when interviewing candidates for a job
- Analyze and project market trends

Skills (psychomotor domain): Refers to manual, physical, or mental tasks that require practice in order to do them successfully.

- Replace the brakes on a delivery truck
- Develop schematics for a building addition
- Build applications for a mobile device
- Process a patient registration form

Attitudes (also called abilities or attributes) (affective domain): Refers to the behaviors through which values, feelings, and emotions are expressed; may also refer to an individual's traits and personal characteristics.[5]

- Pay attention while other people are talking
- Respect other people's point of view even if you disagree
- Present a professional image when meeting clients
- Help others succeed by providing advice, encouragement, and feedback

You may be thinking that some of these examples could fall into more than one category, and you'd be right. Isn't "pay attention while others are talking" an ability as well as a skill? Doesn't "write research reports" require both knowledge and writing skills? In practice, Dr. Bloom's definitions are seldom followed rigorously or even consistently. Still, an understanding of the differences between types of learning helps you develop useful competency models, write job descriptions, develop performance standards, and, as you'll see in Chapter 7, develop learning objectives and select learning methods.

Four Types of Competency Models

Although there is naturally a great deal of overlap, one way to look at competency models is to think about them in terms of four broad categories: core, functional, job, and leadership.

Core competencies (also known as *generic* or *organizational* competencies) describe the competencies that everyone in the organization must have. Those core competencies include an understanding of what the organization is and what it does: its mission, values, products, services, and strategies. Pay special attention to developing your core competency model. That

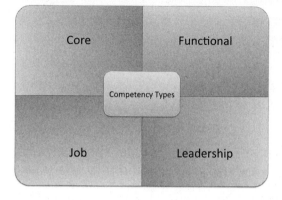

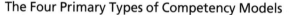

The Four Primary Types of Competency Models

model describes the kind of organization you want to be, and it can help transform your organization's culture.

One distinguishing characteristic of a learning organization is that the core competencies typically include communication, collaboration, problem-solving, and critical-thinking skills; innovation and creativity; willingness to learn, flexibility, and an open mind; respect for others; teamwork; computer and social media literacy; cross-cultural understanding; integrity; and more.

Functional competencies, sometimes referred to as *job family* competencies, are those needed by everyone who works in a particular department, unit, or team, such as sales, IT, marketing, design, customer service, accounting, finance, management, or human resources. For example, all employees in marketing need an understanding of that functional area's reason for being—its role and purpose in the organization—and strategic goals, along with detailed knowledge of the products the organization sells or the services it provides.

Functional competencies are somewhat common across a specific industry or type of organization: Sales competencies for a software company differ to some degree from those for a real estate development company or a company that manufactures harvesters. A city government or a hospital needs certain unique competencies that a chain of retail stores does not. Those competencies can be seen at the website www.CareerOneStop.com, sponsored by the U.S. Department of Labor, Employment and Training Administration, which provides generic functional competency models for many different types of organizations.

Job competencies are those someone needs to carry out a specific job within a specific functional area of the organization. Job competencies describe the specific skills, knowledge, and abilities/attitudes/attributes that top performers in that job possess. They guide your recruiting and selection efforts, and they create the standard against which an employee's performance can be measured.

Job competencies differ to some degree from organization to organization, function to function, and job to job. Although all salespeople share the need for certain skills, such as negotiating and the ability to close a sale, global sales requires somewhat different competencies than domestic sales, sales to the China market may require some different competencies than sales to the Asian-Pacific market, and sales of products requires some different competencies than sales of services. In fact, the same job in different functional areas may require different competencies: Although all nurses must have certain skills, knowledge, and abilities, nursing in a pediatric ward and an operating theater require additional competencies that are specific to those jobs.

Leadership competencies describe the competencies high-performing executives, managers, team leaders, and others who play leadership roles in the organization possess. Those competencies typically include self-confidence, the ability to make decisions and commit to a course of action, visioning skills, an open mind, sensitivity to the needs of others, professional judgment, and the ability to be a role model.

Like core competencies, your leaders' competencies help shape your organization's culture: The kind of leaders you have help characterize the kind of organization you are. Many consultants and organizations have developed leadership competency models you can draw on as you develop your own leadership competency models.

Competencies for Today and Tomorrow

The illiterate of the 21st century will not be those who cannot read and write, but those who cannot learn, unlearn, and relearn.[6]

—Psychologist Herbert Gerjuoy

We are currently preparing students for jobs that don't yet exist . . . using technologies that haven't yet been invented . . . to solve problems we don't even know are problems yet.[7]

—Karl Fisch and Scott McLeod

Competency models have changed since McClelland's day. According to the Institute of the Future, rote and repetitive tasks are increasingly automated, eliminating certain functions and jobs and creating others. We now rely on varied and sophisticated technological tools that are changing how we communicate as well as when, where, and how we work. Success in the increasingly globalized environment that the new technologies and new business models have made possible requires an understanding of, and respect for, diversity. These forces of change are causing us to build new competency models for existing jobs, jobs that didn't exist when many of us joined the workforce, and jobs that are likely to be needed in the future. And one competency is fundamental to every competency model: learning.

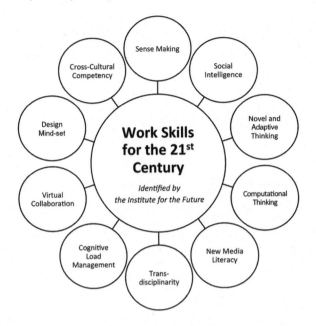

Work Skills for the 21st Century

Identified by the Institute for the Future

Sense Making · Social Intelligence · Novel and Adaptive Thinking · Computational Thinking · New Media Literacy · Trans-disciplinarity · Cognitive Load Management · Virtual Collaboration · Design Mind-set · Cross-Cultural Competency

Competencies for the Twenty-First Century

A great deal of work is currently being done to develop new frameworks that describe the learning-related competencies that are needed as we move deeper into the new century. An example is the framework resulting from research by the Institute for the Future (IFTF), an independent strategic research group that seeks to "identify emerging trends and discontinuities that will transform global society and the global marketplace." In its report, *Future Work Skills 2020*, the IFTF identifies 10 key work skills needed in the next decade, all of which are learning-related competencies.[8]

1. **Sense Making.** The ability to "listen" beyond the words to understand "the deeper meaning or significance of what is being expressed"; the higher-level skills that distinguish humans from machines and are critical to decision making.

2. **Social Intelligence.** The ability to negotiate complex social relationships, assess other people's feelings, and connect with others deeply and directly, which are essential

competencies not only for collaboration and building relationships but also for working with people in different cultures and settings.

3. **Novel and Adaptive Thinking.** To use a cliché, proficiency at thinking outside the box, the ability to come up with innovative solutions and new ways of doing things; also, the ability to adapt to changing and unexpected circumstances.

4. **Computational Thinking.** The ability to understand and use vast amounts of data.

5. **New Media Literacy.** The ability to assess, use, and develop content for new forms of media; the ability to use media to engage and persuade others.

6. **Transdisciplinarity.** The ability to understand and apply concepts across multiple disciplines; curiosity and a willingness to learn beyond a single specialized field to be able to work in multidisciplinary teams.

7. **Cognitive Load Management.** Faced with massive amounts of information, the ability to avoid cognitive overload by using available tools and techniques to identify and focus on what's important.

8. **Virtual Collaboration.** The ability to engage, lead, communicate, collaborate, and negotiate as a member of a team with members scattered in different locations, which is essential as more and more people work remotely.

9. **Design Mind-Set.** The ability to recognize that different tasks may require different thinking and to make changes in processes and environments that make it easier to achieve specific outcomes.

10. **Cross-Cultural Competency.** The ability to build relationships and work successfully with people who are different from ourselves.

Similar work is being done by other organizations, including the Partnership for 21st Century Learning (P21), a broad coalition made up of education nonprofits, foundations, and businesses working together "to serve as a catalyst to position 21st century readiness at the center of US K12 education by building collaborative partnerships among education, business, community, and government leaders."[9] You'll find more about P21 in Chapter 9.

Developing Competency Models

Do not reinvent the wheel. Use a research-based competency library as the foundation.[10]

—*J. Evelyn Orr, Craig Sneltjes, and Guangrong Dai*

The "shelf life" of a competency model has diminished. Frequent reorganizations change job roles and make existing job descriptions and competency models obsolete. Competency models are often needed for new and critical jobs, even though there are few employees with experience in these jobs and fewer still who could be considered outstanding performers.[11]

—*Dr. Richard S. Mansfield*

An experienced tailor can use the same basic pattern over and over to create the same style of suit. But she doesn't use the pattern the same way for all her customers, because they are not all the same. Some are tall, some short, some thin, and some plump. Some prefer pinstripes, others plain grey broadcloth. But the pattern serves an important purpose: It means that the tailor does not have to begin making every suit from scratch. It's a starting place, a framework she adapts to make a suit that is a perfect fit for each individual.

In the same way, existing competency models and frameworks provide a pattern that serves as a starting place for developing your own. Developing valid, useful competency models is a complex, long-term, often costly process that requires collecting, analyzing, and validating a substantial amount of information. Drawing from well-researched and validated competency frameworks means that you don't have to start from scratch.

Not all organizations have the expertise to develop competency models on their own. But even if you enlist the help of experienced professionals who have the right tools and access to the latest research, it is vital that you and others in your organization, including senior leaders, managers, HR staff, and employees at all levels, actively participate in the process. Organization-wide engagement helps ensure that the resulting models accurately describe the competencies that your employees need and helps develop a common understanding of the critical behaviors that affect the organization's success.

Identifying Critical Competencies

When you develop competency models, you seek to identify the critical competencies that your employees must have for you to achieve your mission and strategic goals and be the kind of organization you want to be.

A simple way to get started is to make a list with four columns, one for each type of competency: core, functional, job, and leadership. Don't worry about fitting items neatly into the categories. Just write down every competency you think your organization needs, without stopping to evaluate or organize the items.

When you run out of things to write down, review your lists. Move items from one category to another if that seems appropriate. Add any items that occur to you, and cross out any competencies that seem unimportant. Then circle the 10–15 competencies within each category that appear to be the most critical for success. From there, you can continue along the path to developing your organization's competency models.

When you make your lists, consider the following.

Core Competencies

> I believe the people I hire must have one thing: an open mind. They must have minds that are open to everything and attached to nothing. Once you find people with the right attitude, you can always train for skills. So you hire for attitude and train for skills, you don't go the other way around.[12]
>
> —*Savio Chan*

Ask, "For us to achieve our mission and strategic goals and to be the kind of organization we want to be, what does *everyone* in the organization need to know and be able to do? What abilities/attitudes/attributes must all our employees, at all levels, possess?"

Think carefully about your core competencies—they give you a chance to effect change in the organization's culture. As you move toward becoming a learning organization, your structure will become flatter and more flexible, with a greatly reduced hierarchy and fewer boundaries. Certain core competencies will be increasingly important, including coaching, facilitating, collaborating, peer leadership, interpersonal skills, innovation, and—it goes without saying—learning.

Functional Competencies. Think about the functional areas—departments, units, or teams—you need to achieve your mission and strategic goals: accounting, HR, technology, operations, marketing, sales, customer service, product development, and so on. Ask, "In addition to the core competencies, what do all the employees in this functional area need to know or be able to do? What characteristics do they need to possess?"

When identifying functional competencies, look beyond the present. Consider your long-term goals, and think about how your industry is likely to change. In addition to the functional competencies you need right now, what new competencies might you need in the future?

Job Competencies.   For each job or position in each functional area, ask, "What specific competencies do these employees need for the department, unit, or team to achieve its goals?" A customer service representative may need excellent listening skills, patience, the ability to speak clearly, and the ability to use the relevant technology. A proposal writer may need to know how to read a request for proposals, gather information, and write proposals that clearly address the client's need.

Continue to look forward as you think about job competency models. What new jobs might you need done in the future to meet long-term goals and keep up with change? What competencies would people need for those jobs?

Leadership Competencies.   Ask, "What core competencies do leaders in this organization need for us to achieve our goals and be the kind of organization we want to be? What specific competencies do leaders in each functional area need?" For example, all managers must be able to delegate, communicate clearly, collaborate with others, and provide useful feedback to employees. Some managers may need to be able to do financial analysis, write reports, or do assessments.

Tips for Developing Useful Competency Models

Depending on the size and complexity of your organization, developing competency models can be a time-consuming, complex process. For that reason, many organizations seek the help of consultants or companies that have the necessary tools and expertise.

But whether you develop your competency models on your own or work with a consultant, consider the following:

Use competency libraries thoughtfully. Make sure the competencies you draw on are well researched and validated, written in easy-to-understand language, and unambiguous. Evaluate generic models carefully, and make whatever changes are necessary to ensure that they are relevant and accurate for your organization.

Make sure your competency models are valid. Base changes to generic models and models for new jobs on research, not assumptions. Do your own research if you can, or work with an expert to discover the critical KSAs that make a person successful, and validate your findings.

Focus on critical competencies. You're likely to come up with long lists of desirable competencies for a particular function or job. That's a good starting place. Then edit the list to the 10–15 competencies that are the most essential for carrying out the function or job successfully.

Review competency models often, and update them when things change. Organizational culture, goals, and strategies change; functions and jobs change; researchers make new discoveries about what makes someone a top performer. Treat competency models like living documents. Review them regularly, and review them again when you make significant organizational changes. Keep your models relevant by making them accessible to everyone in the organization and encouraging the people closest to a function or job to recommend improvements.

Keep the big picture in mind. It's easy to get lost in the weeds when trying to figure out what your employees need to know and be able to do. Remember that the purpose of developing and implementing competency models is to help your organization succeed. Keep asking questions like, "What do people need to know and be able to do so that we can achieve our vision, mission, and strategic goals?" and "What knowledge, skills, and abilities do people need so that we can differentiate ourselves from our competitors?"

Using Your Competency Models

Needs assessment is a diagnostic process that relies on data collection, collaboration, and negotiation to identify and understand gaps in learning and performance and to determine future actions.[13]

—*Kavita Gupta, Catherine M. Sleezer, and Darlene F. Russ-Eft*

One reason competency models are important is that they help you keep HR practices consistent across the organization. For one thing, they guide your recruiting and hiring efforts. As McClelland and others found, competencies are more effective predictors of success in a job than traditional selection criteria, such as tests, degrees and credentials, and work experience. After all, holding a MBA or having worked in the investment field for five years is no guarantee that someone will be able to succeed as a financial analyst in your organization.

Hiring is not the only—or necessarily the best—way to ensure that your organization has the competencies it needs to achieve its goals. Recruiting and hiring is costly, and even top candidates rarely have the ideal skill set for a specific role, function, or job.

That brings us to another key reason to develop competency models—to do the needs assessments that help you determine what people need to learn. A needs assessment is a tool for identifying the gaps between the competencies people have and the ones they need, determining which gaps can addressed by learning, identifying development opportunities, establishing priorities, and more.

The task of conducting an organization-wide needs assessment can be daunting. It is likely to take many months and a great deal of work to complete. But a comprehensive needs assessment will save your organization money, time, wasted effort, and a great deal of grief. As we discussed in Chapter 3, not all competency gaps can be filled by learning. For example, assessment results may make it clear that the best way to close a gap is by seeking candidates with certain critical core or job competencies or by changing your procedures, organizational structure, or physical layout so that employees can perform at their best.

The Needs Assessment Process

> A training analysis is conducted ultimately to identify what areas of knowledge or behaviors that training needs to accomplish. . . . The analysis considers what results the organization needs from the learner, what knowledge and skills the learner presently has and usually concludes with identifying what knowledge and skills the learner must gain (the "performance gap").[14]
> —*Carter McNamara*

Conducting a needs assessment requires gathering and analyzing information from various sources. Those sources typically include:

- Data from sales records, financial reports, performance evaluation forms, emerging trend reports, and other documents that show increases or decreases in productivity, performance, and profitability.

- Surveys and questionnaires administered to customers, employees, and others, which can help you identify patterns that indicate a need for change. To be useful, these instruments need to be carefully designed to elicit specific information, clearly worded so the questions are unambiguous, and administered to a relatively large group. You might also need to offer an incentive of some kind to encourage people to complete and return the survey or questionnaire.

- Assessments and tests that measure people's attitudes, what they already know, and what skills they possess. Like surveys and questionnaires, tests and assessments need to be carefully designed for the results to be valid.

- Observation of performance or the results of performance, which can indicate how well an employee (or a team) is able to meet performance standards. Observations take time, and the validity of the results depends to a great degree on the observer's ability to be a fly on the wall and not interfere in any way or make the people being observed uncomfortable, which can cause them to change their behavior.

- Interviews and focus groups, which can help discover what people see as competency gaps, possible reasons for those gaps, and ideas for change. Like observation, this information collection method can take a great deal of time. For the results to be useful, you need a skilled interviewer or facilitator, a diverse group of participants who can offer differing perspectives, and relevant questions that are designed to elicit the desired information.

Identify Root Causes and Set Priorities

The results of your needs assessment may point to competency gaps that learning programs could fill. The operative word in that sentence is *may*. Before jumping to the conclusion that learning is the solution, consider these questions:

What's the root cause? Learning will only muddy the waters and waste resources if the gap is caused by the organizational culture or structure, inadequate resources, ineffective or contradictory policies and procedures, unrealistic expectations, a significant mismatch between the employee and the organization or the job, or other factors.

How important is it to address the gap? You can't realistically attempt to close every competency gap—nor should you. Focus on gaps that must be closed because of legal mandates, safety, drops in sales, dissatisfied employees or customers, product defects, cost overruns, organizational reputation, changes in strategic goals, or other important factors. Then do a cost-benefit analysis of closing those gaps. In some cases, you may find that the cost of using learning to close a specific competency gap outweighs the benefits.

Examples of Competency Models

Core Competencies

Communication

- Listens actively
- Expresses oneself clearly verbally and in writing
- Asks questions as needed to confirm understanding

Teamwork

- Works well with others and builds constructive relationships
- Asks for help when necessary
- Contributes ideas and shares information
- Gives and shares credit for ideas and successes
- Takes responsibility

- Takes a win-win approach to problems
- Offers assistance to colleagues

Problem Solving

- Takes ownership of problems
- Collects relevant information
- Identifies root causes
- Uses brainstorming to come up with possible solutions

Interpersonal Skills

- Treats others with respect, trust, and dignity
- Is considerate of other people's needs and feelings

Self-Direction

- Organizes work and manages priorities effectively
- Finds efficient ways of accomplishing goals
- Meets deadlines
- Learns from mistakes

Flexibility

- Willing to take on new challenges and try new ways of doing things
- Adapts well to change

Functional Competencies for a Sales Team

Product

- Understands our products
- Analyzes the competition

Prospecting

- Continually seeks opportunities to develop new business
- Does customer and industry research
- Develops sales plans and strategies

Customers

- Identifies target customers
- Builds relationships with customers
- Identifies customer needs and buying criteria
- Explains why our products meet customer needs better than those of the competition
- Able to build a value case
- Able to close sales

Account Management

- Organizes and manages contacts and accounts effectively
- Creates schedules
- Achieves sales targets
- Prepares reports

Job Competencies for a Learning Professional

Learning Methods

- Understands the different ways that adults learn
- Has a good knowledge of the various formal and informal learning methods available

Instructional Design

- Conducts needs assessments

- Develops learning goals

- Designs individual learning programs, workshops and seminars, and e-learning programs to meet specific goals

- Develops program materials and validates courses

- Assesses outcomes

Deliver In-Person and Virtual Learning Programs

- Effectively plans and prepares to deliver learning

- Engages learners

- Presents material clearly and answers learners' questions

- Follows up on learning programs

Leadership Competencies

Leadership

- Sets the example

- Engenders trust

- Influences others

- Sets and clearly communicates values, vision, and strategic goals

- Values diversity and promotes a positive culture by treating everyone with respect

- Takes the initiative

- Creates and leads high-performance teams

- Provides feedback, coaching, and career development to employees
- Manages change

Decision Making

- Willingly elicits others' ideas and perspectives during the decision-making process
- Collects all relevant information before making a decision
- Able to assess situations and make decisions quickly in times of crisis
- Clearly communicates decisions and the reasons they were made

Professionalism

- Demonstrates integrity
- Acknowledges and learns from mistakes
- Seeks opportunities for professional development
- Manages priorities efficiently
- Builds constructive relationships
- Delivers on commitments

Project Management

- Sets goals, establishes time lines and schedules, and prepares budgets
- Delegates work effectively
- Works with team members and others to keep projects on track and effectively resolve problems, disagreements, and conflict

To Consider: What critical functional competencies does your organization need to achieve its goals? What core competencies does everyone in the organization need for you to become a learning organization? What competencies do you want your leaders to have? What competencies might people need in the future?

What's Next: Learning initiatives and learning programs are an important element in strengthening your employees' competencies and helping them increase their value to the organization by developing new competencies. In the next chapter, we'll discuss how to choose the right learning methods to meet individual and organizational goals.

Selecting the Right Learning Methods

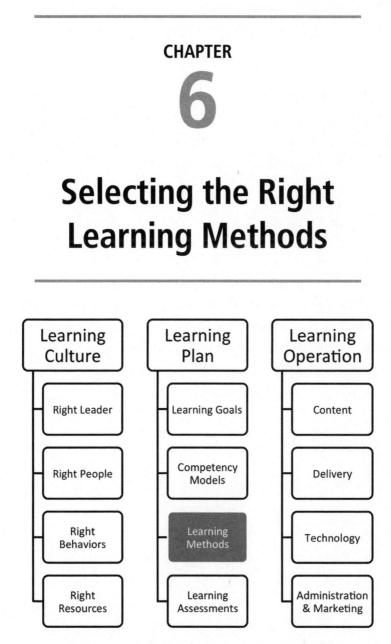

Sarder Framework: Building the Learning Organization

We all learn best in our own ways. Some people do better studying one subject at a time, while some do better studying three things at once. Some people do best studying in [a] structured, linear way, while others do best jumping around, "surrounding" a subject.[1]

—*Bill Gates*

In my second book, *Effective Learning Methods*, I tell the story of a friend who took up ballet in her late thirties. "Everyone was expected to simply watch the instructor, then follow his movements," she told me. "But this alone didn't work for me. I had to follow his movements, then take the time to run them through my brain. I had to say to myself, 'I'm going to raise my right foot, followed by my left, then turn.' Initially, I was frustrated because my method was slow, but it worked for me."[2]

My friend needed to synthesize her instructor's movements before she could do the steps. That was her way of learning. Another person might have learned simply by watching the instructor and then trying to do what he did. Still another might have had to take copious notes while watching to be able to understand how one step flowed into another.

People have different learning styles and preferences. The best learning programs consider those differences, and they also consider differences in what is being taught. An understanding of the various ways in which people learn helps you choose the method or combination of methods that is best for a given person and situation.

Formal versus Informal Learning

Formal learning is what we typically associate with the word *learning*—we spent most of the first two decades of our lives in classrooms, after all, and most of us have continued our formal

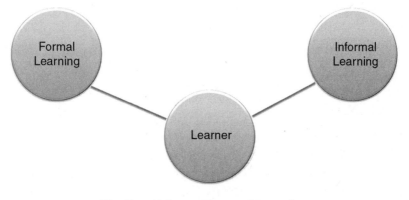

The Two Primary Types of Learning

learning after college by taking workshops, seminars, and self-study courses.

Formal learning is carefully designed to achieve specific outcomes. Those outcomes are usually stated in the form of objectives: "When they complete this program, the learners will be able to. . . ." The success of the program can be measured by asking, "How well did participants meet the objectives?"

There are many benefits to formal learning programs for both organizations and learners. For example, formal learning gives organizations a great deal of control over the content people learn, as well the way in which they learn it, and it can be structured so that all participants learn the same content in the same way. But there are downsides: Formal learning programs can be time-consuming to develop and costly to purchase. Employees need to take time away from their jobs to participate. Without careful planning, even well-designed programs may not do a very good job of achieving the desired outcomes.

Much of our most valuable learning is the *informal learning* that takes place as we go about our daily activities, often unaware that we are learning. We learn informally by looking up information; by reading books, articles, and documents; through social media; from informational podcasts and video presentations; in discussion groups; from mentors and coaches; as we engage in problem solving; and in many other ways. Unlike formal learning, informal learning costs little or nothing and requires little or no development time. It's far more flexible—content can be assembled and disseminated quickly to the people who need it, and learners can discover content on their own.

With access to the Internet and social media, many of today's workers prefer informal learning to learning through more structured programs. One disadvantage, however, is that organizations have little control over what, how, and when their employees learn informally. Informal learning also works best when people feel motivated to learn and have opportunities to apply what they learn.

Five Primary Learning Methods

There are five primary learning methods. A good learning organization uses all of them, often in combination. At NetCom Learning, we felt that it was essential to promote a learning environment that reached out to every employee and that using these five main learning methods was the best way to ensure that every employee had a path to follow. The result of this strategy was a 20 percent growth in productivity.

Although they differ in important ways, effective learning methods share certain common characteristics:

- They are designed or selected as the best fit for the specific situation.
- The content is relevant to the organization and the learner.
- They are appropriate for what is being taught.

Primary Learning Methods

- They meet the needs of people with differing individual learning styles.

- They offer ample opportunities for reflection, practice, and application.

Classroom Learning

Traditionally, the words *training* and *learning* meant learning with a group of people in a classroom. Classroom learning is by definition synchronous: The learners and the instructor must be in the same place at the same time. Today, that place might be a virtual rather than physical space, but it's a classroom nevertheless.

The percentage of learning delivered in corporate classrooms has been dropping. *Training* magazine's "2013 Training

Industry Report" found that not even 44 percent of training hours were delivered by a live instructor in a classroom, although the percentage was slightly higher in smaller organizations.[3]

There are numerous advantages to classroom learning. The great benefit is the face-to-face interaction that lets students ask questions, explore issues, and share ideas, which means that they learn from one another as well as from the instructor. Learners can engage in role plays and simulations to practice new behaviors; they can collaborate with others to apply what they learn by analyzing a situation and coming up with their own conclusions or solutions.

Classroom learning also can be far more flexible than some other types of formal learning, such as e-learning programs. If skilled instructors are available, a course can be put together somewhat quickly, for not much more than the cost of the instructor and learners' time. Content can be easily tailored to meet the needs of a specific group, even at the last minute, even on the spot.

The obvious disadvantage is that classroom learning requires learners to free up significant blocks of time, and it can take some doing to arrange a time when all the participants can be available. Because different instructors may teach the same class and instructors may customize the content to meet specific needs, not everyone will learn the same things in the same way.

Classroom training is not the best choice for presenting purely factual information or mechanical skills. It's also not everyone's preferred way to learn—some people learn best on their own instead of in a group. When there are widely differing levels of experience, skills, and knowledge in a class, some participants will move ahead quickly and others may fall behind.

Finally, except for impromptu courses, classroom learning programs such as workshops can be expensive and time-consuming to develop. Off-the-shelf courses can be difficult or impossible to customize, and the one-size-fits-all model might not meet all participants' specific needs.

Coaching

> [People] can come to a class and get some skills, but someone needs to reinforce what they learn: "How are you implementing these behaviors? What kinds of actions have you taken?" For the behavior change really to happen, I think there needs to be one-to-one coaching.[4]
>
> —*Jennifer Alesia*

> Coaches who can outline plays on a blackboard are a dime a dozen. The ones who win get inside their players and motivate.[5]
>
> —*Vince Lombardi*

Coaches work one-on-one with individuals, and sometimes with teams, to inspire and energize, help them work through problems and experiment, provide feedback, and encourage them to perform at their personal best. If you play or follow sports, you know that good coaching can mean the difference between mediocre performance and success.

Coaching helps people learn from experience. The coach observes the learners do something, asks questions to help their reflect on what happened, and helps determine what they might try doing differently the next time.

This learning method is usually long term and can be costly in terms of the coach's time. Its great advantage is that a good coach helps learners think for themselves, adapt to new circumstances, and find better and better ways to accomplish their goals.

Not everyone has the patience needed to be a good coach and to be supportive even when the learner doesn't seem to be making much progress. Effective coaches have a good understanding of how to help people learn. They know that simply pointing out flaws and telling people, "Do this, do that, do it this way" isn't very helpful. That kind of coaching can leave the learner feeling frustrated and unwilling to take the risks necessary to learn.

Coaching requires commitment on the part of the learner as well. Learners must agree to be coached and believe the process is of value. They must also be willing to see their blind spots, the faults that others perceive but that they are unaware of themselves.

Mentoring

> *Mentorship* is a word that encapsulates the core of positive networking behavior, which is to find people who are ahead of you and learn from them so that you always raise the level of your game to the people around you.[6]
>
> —*Lewis Schiff*

Mentors, who typically are people with experience in the learner's industry or profession, provide long-term, one-on-one guidance targeted toward a learner's specific needs. Mentoring can be an extremely effective way to pass down lessons learned, insights, values, techniques, and more.

People usually find mentors on their own, seeking out someone they respect, often in the same organization, field, or industry. But mentoring also occurs between peers who meet to share ideas and experiences, and people can learn a great deal from mentors they've never met, by reading books or watching videos that illustrate what people they admire and respect have done to succeed. With hindsight, many people realize that their parents and teachers have been among their most important mentors.

As today's organizations search for ways to help their employees increase their knowledge and improve their skills, some have begun to include mentoring in their learning plans, helping employees connect with mentors within or outside the organization.

There are a number of disadvantages to mentoring. Mentors have no direct responsibility for the person's learning, so individuals are on their own when it comes to determining what advice to follow. The advice mentors gives is based on their own knowledge and experience; learners must be able to sort out what's useful from what might not be relevant or might even lead them down the wrong path.

Mentoring is not a quick fix. It takes place over a relatively long period, sometimes years. Even so, there will come a point at which the person being mentored needs to move on. When that happens, the learner may need to find a comfortable way to end the relationship.

On-the-Job Training

What we have to learn to do, we learn by doing.[7]

—*Aristotle*

We learn by example and by direct experience because there are real limits to the adequacy of verbal instruction.[8]

—*Malcolm Gladwell*

Throughout the ages, people have learned how to do a job by becoming an apprentice, working side by side with bakers, lawyers, tailors, and blacksmiths who passed on their skills and knowledge to the new generation.

According to the U.S. Department of Labor, "Apprenticeship is a combination of on-the-job training and related instruction in which workers learn the practical and theoretical aspects of a highly skilled occupation."[9] In today's organizations, this form of learning is often referred to as "on-the-job training," or simply, OJT. It's the way that many of us learned our jobs.

OJT is one-on-one learning. A novice learns a job little by little by watching an experienced person do the work, asking questions, trying it, getting feedback, and trying it again. Over time, the new person gains the knowledge and experience to do the job on his own.

This learning method has many advantages. For one thing, it's extremely practical. It requires little if any financial outlay, although there are indirect costs, including the time of the learner and of the "instructor," who is typically a manager, supervisor, or experienced employee. People learn what they need to do and exactly how to do it in the environment in which the job is done, so the learning is directly relevant and can be put to use immediately. Experts agree that learning by doing can be the most effective learning method for many people.

But no learning method is perfect, and OJT has some distinct disadvantages. Effective OJT is more than simply having a new employee shadow an experienced person for a few days. It should be as carefully planned as any formal learning program, with clearly defined learning objectives and a program of activities designed to meet them. For some jobs, it can take months or even years for people to become proficient; if they are left on their own too soon, they can become frustrated and even make costly mistakes. The person tasked with helping the learner needs to know how to do the job the right way, be able to explain it clearly, have the patience to let the learner stumble through the process and make mistakes, and provide the feedback and support necessary for the person to learn.

Self-Study

The benefit of learning on your own is that you can explore different ways of thinking, and you can go through difficult concepts on your own without help.[10]

—*Cherry*

Self-study, or self-learning, can be formal learning, carefully designed to achieve specific objectives. It can be informal learning, such as reading and learning from others. What the various forms of self-learning have in common is this: Learners work on their own, at their own pace and at a time of their choosing, to gain knowledge or practice skills they need to carry out their jobs, to improve their performance, or to move forward in their career—or just because they are curious.

Formal Self-Study. A structured self-study program, well designed to meet specific objectives, can be an extremely effective way for people to learn. It can be a very cost-effective way to deliver learning to large numbers of people, especially when the topic does not require interaction with others and it is important for everyone to learn the same content in the same way. The logistical problems associated with classroom learning become moot—you don't have to bring a group together with a live instructor in a physical or virtual place—and there are no travel costs. Learners can usually work at their own pace whenever they choose, take whatever time they need to complete the program, and repeat sections of the program as often as they need to.

Until the last part of the twentieth century, formal self-learning was typically delivered via printed self-study workbooks. But print programs, the cheapest to develop, are being used less and less often; today's learners are increasingly more comfortable with a computer than with paper and pencil.

Today, most self-learning programs are delivered on a computer, tablet, or mobile device in the form of e-learning, Internet-based learning, podcasts and video presentations, and most recently, massive open online courses (MOOCs), which make free learning content available to anyone who wants to take a course.

A good podcast or video presentation provides information clearly, with examples that help people learn and, perhaps, suggestions for applying the learning. But the best self-learning programs provide the interactivity that keeps learners engaged and lets them practice what they are learning in real or simulated situations. Today's electronic self-learning programs can be very engaging—many have compelling graphics, video, or animation, and many are designed as games. They are relatively easy to update, to customize for the organization, and to tailor to individual needs. Electronic forms of self-learning also offer something unique: Program administrators can easily track learners' progress and measure their success in achieving the learning objectives.

Like any other learning method, formal self-learning programs, whether print or electronic, have drawbacks. Some learners never finish, at least not without a lot of prodding. Even the best off-the-shelf programs may not be a good fit for the organization and its learners, and highly customized e-learning programs can be expensive and time-consuming to develop. Podcasts and video presentations, although relatively inexpensive to produce, may be a good way to convey information to large groups, but they offer few if any opportunities for interaction and practice.

Informal Self-Study

Every man who knows how to read has it in his power to magnify himself, to multiply the ways in which he exists, to make his life full, significant and interesting.[11]

—*Aldous Huxley*

We have a manager's learning group. We assign a book and then get together in groups to work through business problems, applying the things we learned in the book. We also ask people to present to the rest of the group, so teaching is part of the learning path.[12]

—*Heather Bennett*

Informal self-learning lets people take charge of their own learning by deciding what to learn, when to learn it, and how to learn it. The most common, and still the most valuable, form is *reading*, a time-honored form of self-learning that offers new knowledge and ideas, different perspectives, and new ways of seeing the world. Not only are books valuable repositories of knowledge that teach, inspire, and make life meaningful, but also researchers have found that reading can have a powerful effect on shaping the brain.

Reading is an individual activity, and many people learn best that way. People can read whenever they want and wherever they happen to be, using print books, e-books, print or online magazine and journal articles, and even blog posts to learn how to do something, learn about something, or learn what others think—or simply immerse themselves in someone else's world for a time. Free libraries and the wealth of material available on the Internet keep the cost extremely low.

The primary disadvantage to reading as a learning method is that not everyone is a reader. Unless someone loves reading, as many of us do, a reader may need to be highly motivated to take time out of a busy schedule to read. For that reason, study groups, where all members read the same material and meet to discuss it, can extend the value of reading in an organizational setting.

Today, social media is rapidly becoming an increasingly valuable source of informal self-learning, helping people learn continuously at work and in their personal lives. In brief chunks of time, learners can get information, answers to questions, and insights from a wide range of people all over the world and share their learning with others. They can keep up with topics that interest them by subscribing to feeds, participating in forums, and joining groups. There are cautions, however. Learners need to be aware that not everything they find will be accurate, complete, or relevant, so they need to filter and verify social media content. Also, to keep social media from becoming a constant distraction, it's important for people to limit the number of feeds and alerts they receive and resist the temptation to browse social media sites whenever they feel bored.

Informal learning can take place anywhere, at any time. Much of the most valuable informal learning within organizations happens while people are engaged in meetings and conversations. They learn by asking questions, sharing information, grappling with problems, and helping one another figure out how to do things. Learning organizations recognize the value of these every-day interactions and do what they can to encourage them.

What's the Most Effective Learning Method?

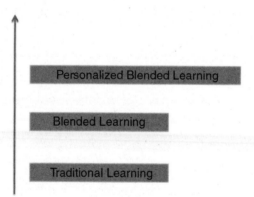

Customizing the Learning Method

Blended learning . . . applies a mix of [learning methods] to teach, support, and sustain the skills needed for top perform-ance. . . . The tried-and-true traditional learning methods are combined with new technology to create a synergistic, dynamic learning structure that can propel learning to new heights.[13]

—Caroline Gray

There is rarely one best way to meet a learning goal. Top learning organizations combine methods to fit the needs of the organization, the learner, and the situation. Learning professionals refer to that combination as "blended learning."

Blended learning is a customized approach that takes into consideration such factors as the learning goals and objectives, how individuals prefer to learn, where learners are located, the budget, the time people have available for learning, and the urgency of closing a competency gap. When carefully planned, blended learning, especially when it is personalized for the individual, can be the most cost-effective way to use resources and give both the organization and the learners the maximum amount of control over the learning process.

There are countless ways to combine learning methods to meet specific goals and needs. Here are a few examples:

- Use self-learning programs and coaching to support on-the-job training.

- Assign a series of readings, podcasts, or video presentations to help people prepare for, or to follow up, a workshop or seminar.

- Help people form study groups to share and explore the learning from self-learning programs.

- After people complete a formal learning program, have them participate in an online forum or discussion group where they can post their experiences in applying the learning, ask one another questions, and share ideas and best practices.

What Drives the Selection of Learning Methods?

I believe experiential learning is the most effective, but everybody has a different learning style. Some people can learn by a watching a video, but not everybody's going to be successful with that. It's important that we're not looking at learning as, "Okay everybody's to learn this way." We're trying to focus on giving people an experience that has a combination of online and offline and letting them figure out what's best for them.[14]

—*Laurie Carey*

Which learning method or combination would be most effective in a given situation depends on a number of learning method selection drivers.

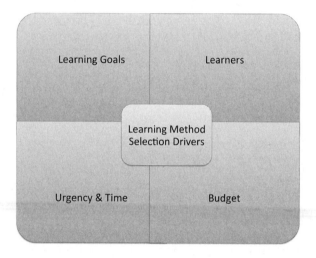

The Four Primary Learning Method Selection Drivers

Learning Goals. What are the organization, team, and individual goals that the learning program is intended to achieve? No matter how interesting, engaging, or fun your learning programs might be, they are a waste of resources, including time and effort, unless they help people get where they want to go.

Urgency and Learners' Available Time. How quickly does a competency gap need to be closed? Do learners need to get up to speed on new technology? Pass a licensing exam? Meet a deadline? If so, an off-the-shelf program or other method that requires little if any development and customization might be the best choice. How much time do learners have available for learning activities? Can they be spared from the workplace long enough to take a class, or would an e-learning program reinforced with coaching or a study group be a better option? Be realistic when thinking about learners' available time. If the time pressures are too great, learners are likely to skip classes or fail to complete self-study programs.

Budget. How much money do you have available? What are the cost constraints? A customized e-learning program with long-term coaching program might be the best option for a given individual or group, but if your budget is limited or the cost outweighs the benefits, a well-designed off-the-shelf course combined with informal study groups may be a good alternative. If a large number of widely dispersed people need the learning, a self-learning program supplemented with an online forum might be the most practical. MOOCs supplemented with assigned reading may be a more cost-effective way to help people achieve the goals than sending them to public classes or reimbursing them for college tuition. Be careful not to compromise too much, however. It's better to spend more money on an effective program than to save money on one that doesn't do the job.

The Learners. What do people need to learn—facts, skills, information, techniques, methods, or ideas? What are their learning styles and preferences? How much experience do they have? How many learners are there, and where are they located? The answers to all those questions affect your choice of learning methods. Consider the following:

- Different methods work best for different types of learning. Team-building or interpersonal communication skills might be best addressed in a physical or virtual classroom, where learners have face-to-face interaction. E-learning might be the most cost-effective way to help people learn how to prepare a budget. Sales techniques might be learned on the job with the help of a coach.

- There's no such thing as a typical learner. Visual learners learn best when information is presented through pictures, diagrams, demonstrations, and other visual media or through reading and writing. Auditory learners tend to remember more of what they hear than what they see, and they learn well by listening and talking. Kinesthetic learners prefer doing to listening or watching, so they benefit most from hands-on learning activities. Some people learn best in groups, while others prefer to learn on their own. Using a variety of learning methods helps ensure that people with differing styles and preferences are able to learn.

- Consider what the learners already know and are able to do. People who are already knowledgeable about a topic or are proficient in a topic or a skill need to go well beyond the basics for the learning to be of value to them. Experienced people may be able to learn well on their own, with little guidance, so self-learning, coaching, and mentoring may be good choices. On the other hand, people who are new to a topic, a job, or a skill may need the help and support of an instructor or coach.

- Think about where the learners are located. When inter-action is needed, a class might not be practical if learners are scattered around the globe, but webinars with live instructors combined with virtual study groups might work just fine.

Putting the Learning to Use

Learning is about building the capacity to create that which you previously couldn't create. It's ultimately related to actions, which information is not.[15]

—Peter Senge

"Practice isn't the thing you do once you're good. It's the thing you do that makes you good."[16]

—Malcolm Gladwell

Many people learn because they love the process of learning. There's nothing wrong with that. You can enjoy learning Turkish even though you never plan to visit Turkey or take an acting class even though you have no desire to go on the stage. The act of learning always challenges you. It always enriches your life in some way. But for your organization's investment in learning to pay off, people need to apply that learning. How to ensure that happens is among a learning organization's biggest challenges. The reasons include the following.

People are sent to learning programs that are not relevant to their jobs. A customer service manager signs her staff up for a writing skills class even though they never need to write on the job, or a team leader in research and development decides that all team members should take a course in presentation techniques even though they never make presentations. Not only do people seldom learn much when they take unnecessary courses, but also what they do learn quickly fades away because it's not being used.

People take courses that have little to do with their jobs or career paths. "That sounds like fun," a sales rep might think when the announcement of a course on Web design appears in the company newsletter, without considering how learning to design

Web pages might be useful either now or in the future. Without a clear purpose and opportunities to apply the learning, the skills are likely to fade quickly.

The learning is no longer necessary. For various reasons, changes in policies, strategic goals, product lines, and organizational structure may make the knowledge or skills someone learns unnecessary. It's not unusual for a learning program to go on as scheduled even though a significant change is right on the horizon—or has even taken place. Although some of that learning may be transferable, much of it is likely to be lost.

People have no time to apply the learning. Everyone is so busy these days that it's hard to find time to practice new skills or try out new ways of doing things. When there is a lot of time pressure to get things done, learners may default to the old way so that they don't feel they are falling behind, and the new learning may be quickly forgotten.

The learners receive little or no support. Even the managers and supervisors who encouraged the learning in the first place may be so uncomfortable with change that they refuse to let people do things differently and even punish them for making mistakes. Peers may resist or even challenge someone's efforts to change. It's almost impossible for people to put their learning to use without the support of others.

The organization does not reinforce and reward the learning. Learning is hard work, and applying the learning is even harder. When their efforts and successes are ignored, people may easily become discouraged and let the learning slip away.

Learning organizations recognize these challenges and take steps to address them. They use learning plans to make sure learning programs and activities are relevant to people's jobs and career paths. They review and modify learning plans and programs when significant changes are anticipated or have taken place that might render goals or programs obsolete. They give employees the time and other resources they need to become proficient in using new concepts and techniques. Unafraid of change and committed to learning, everyone from senior managers to the learners' peers remain patient and supportive while they experiment with new ways of doing things. Human resources and compensation policies reinforce and reward the learners' efforts and successes.

To Consider: What are some things you need to think about when selecting learning methods for the people in your organization?

What's Next: There's only one way to know whether you are achieving a goal: by the results. A well-functioning learning organization builds measurement criteria into its goals and evaluates its programs and activities to determine how well they are meeting those goals. Chapter 7 explores how to evaluate your success.

7

Assessing the Results of Your Learning Plan

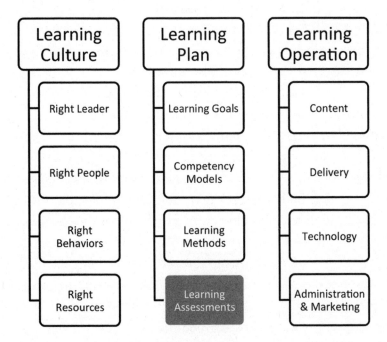

Learning Culture	Learning Plan	Learning Operation
Right Leader	Learning Goals	Content
Right People	Competency Models	Delivery
Right Behaviors	Learning Methods	Technology
Right Resources	Learning Assessments	Administration & Marketing

Sarder Framework: Building the Learning Organization

Evaluation is a constant guard at the gate of failure.[1]

—*Chuck Hodell*

Organizations spend significant amounts of time and effort developing a compelling strategy, defining goals, and articulating a convincing theory of change, without putting into place the infrastructure and support needed to monitor and evaluate whether or not the strategy is actually working.[2]

—*Hallie Preskill and Katelyn Mack*

Suppose the owners of a newly expanded restaurant embark on a campaign to attract customers. They advertise their opening, highlighting a new menu and new chef. They do e-mail marketing, offer incentives, hold special events, and enlist local journalists and food bloggers to write reviews.

Within a few weeks of opening, it's clear that the campaign is a success. The reservation list is full every evening, and some evenings walk-ins hang out at the bar, hoping for a table. The owners congratulate themselves, thank everyone who helped, and begin planning for yet another expansion.

In this situation, success is measured by results: The owners' goal was to attract customers to the expanded restaurant, and the numbers demonstrate that they achieved that goal. But the numbers don't show the entire picture. Which marketing activities were the most successful? How many customers were new, and how many had dined at the restaurant before expansion? How many of the new customers come back? What do customers like most—and least—about the food, the ambience, and the service?

If the restaurant owners want to continue their success and repeat it in a new location, they need answers to those kinds of questions. They need to evaluate every part of their marketing campaign, their menu, their décor, their service, and the restaurant's operations to see what is working and determine what needs to be changed. That's the only way they can keep from being overtaken by the next trendy new restaurant that opens down the street.

The leaders of successful organizations know that the most carefully developed and implemented strategic plans need constant vigilance. That's true of learning plans as well. Learning plans should never be fixed in stone or ignored once they have been implemented. Only by regularly assessing the results of your learning initiatives and programs can you discover the extent to which they are achieving their expected outcomes; if not, why not; and what improvements you can make.

Yet, despite the importance of assessment, many organizations have an on-again, off-again, scattergun approach. Assessment is often way down on the list of priorities and given insufficient resources; as a result, the results are unreliable and lead to little effective change.

It's worth remembering that assessment is itself a learning activity. The thing about learning is that you don't know what you don't know, and it's what you don't know that can lead to wasted resources and disappointing outcomes. Only by gathering and analyzing information from all corners of the organization, and beyond, can you determine what to stop doing and what to change. Only then can you keep on getting better.

Key Assessment Questions

Let's say you train your salespeople. Did their sales numbers go up? That's what really counts. I got a letter recently from one of the managers in the military whose staff was just trained in PMP. He said, "You know what? Our people, only two weeks after your class, they're better already. They are more confident, they are more careful, they are following procedures better, they are getting better results." He can see results with his own eyes.[3]

—*Jeff Furman*

Assessment is essentially a process of asking questions. The overarching question is, "How well are our learning plans achieving what we intended them to achieve?" Let's break that question down into its component parts.

How well is our organizational learning plan helping us build a learning culture? Do we see more information sharing and collaboration between teams and individuals? Have we gotten better at learning from our mistakes? Are people finding opportunities to learn from one another? Can we respond to change more quickly? Are we providing more relevant learning opportunities for employees at all levels, and are employees taking advantage of them? Do people recognize the value of learning for their own and the organization's success? Are they enthusiastic about learning?

How well is our learning plan helping us achieve our organizational goals? To what degree is learning helping us compete more successfully? Improve our productivity? Attract and retain better employees? Be more flexible and innovative? Achieve increased growth and profitability?

How well are team learning plans achieving the expected outcomes? Are teams achieving their goals more effectively and efficiently? Have sales improved? Are we providing better customer service? Have we reduced operational problems and product defects? Attracted and retained more good clients?

How well are individual employees achieving their goals? Are we seeing fewer performance problems? Are more employees achieving or exceeding performance standards? Developing new competencies? Applying learning on the job?

How well is our investment in learning paying off? Are we getting a reasonable return from the money we spend on learning initiatives? On the time our employees spend learning? In what ways is increased learning our bottom line?

If any part of our learning plan is not working, what are the possible reasons? What internal and external factors may be affecting our learning plan? Are our learning goals realistic? Achievable? Have we devoted sufficient resources to learning activities? What changes do we need to make to achieve the desired outcomes more efficiently and effectively?

Assessment Methodologies

> There essentially five ways to evaluate training. The first level is "How is somebody feeling? The second is "Did they acquire the skill and knowledge?" The third is "Were they able to apply the skills and knowledge?" The fourth is "Are you seeing increased sales, improved customer satisfaction?" The most difficult one is ROI, the fifth level. What you're really doing is taking that fourth level, "Have sales improved?" and building a ratio with how much it costs to improve those to reap those additional sales."[4]
>
> —*Michael Tull*

There are many methods for assessing or evaluating the success of an organization's learning activities. The most commonly used method is some version of the model, Four Levels of Evaluation, developed by Professor Donald Kirkpatrick, with Dr. Jack Phillips' ROI addition.

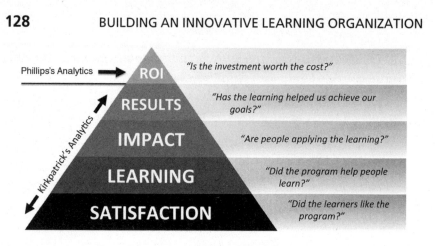

The Five Levels of Evaluation

Level 1. Satisfaction (Did the Learners Like the Program?)

When you contact a company's customer service department, purchase a product online, or use an online service to make a dinner reservation, you're likely to be asked to complete a survey or questionnaire "to help us improve." The questions are similar to those on the questionnaires routinely given to participants right after they complete a course. These assessments are sometimes called "smile sheets" because they seek to discover how learners felt about their experience, not necessarily what they learned.

Smile sheet evaluations are the easiest and least costly to administer, so they are the most commonly used. Although they are very subjective, they can provide useful information as part of a more comprehensive evaluation. For one thing, people usually get more out of learning programs that they enjoy, and when they enjoy a program, they may be more motivated to apply what they learn.

Level 1 evaluations typically ask these kinds of questions:

- Overall, how well did this program meet your needs?

- If the program was conducted by a facilitator or instructor, how well did that person do in helping you learn?

- How well did the learning activities help you master the content or skills?

- How well was the time used? Did any time seem to be wasted?

- Did any information or activities seem unnecessary?

- Did anything seem to be confusing or missing?

- What changes would you suggest to improve this program?

Level 2. Learning (Did the Program Help People Learn?)

"What a great workshop!" someone might say to colleagues at the conclusion of a course. Yet, when questioned about what she learned, she might be hard-pressed to come up with an answer. That's why you need the second level of evaluation, which seeks to determine, "What did people learn? To what extent have they achieved the learning objectives?"

Level 2 evaluations are more difficult to design and administer than Level 1 evaluations. You need a baseline against which to measure change: what people knew or were able to do or what attitudes they had before the learning program. Although Level 2 evaluations provide more useful information than Level 1 evaluations, it's important to note that they measure what people *learned*, not the extent to which they can apply the learning in real-life situations.

The methods for performing a Level 2 evaluation depend on the type of learning that is being measured. Those methods include:

- Written or online tests (knowledge—how well do they know and understand it?)

- Performance tests and observation (skills—how well can they do it?)

- Questionnaires and surveys (attitudes—has there been a change in the way they feel about it?)

- Observation (behavior—has there been a change in the way they do it?)

Level 3. Impact (Are People Applying the Learning?)

> How employees are doing on the job is the best way to measure return on investment for employee training.[5]
>
> —*Jeff Furman*

To use a timeworn cliché, Level 3 evaluations are where the rubber meets the road. Successful learning programs effect change. That change can be seen in the way people go about their work and in the results of that work: Their business writing has improved; they are better at diagnosing product defects; they close more sales. Yet, time and time again, learning professionals hear some version of this common complaint: "That program was a waste of time and money. Hasn't made a bit of difference."

Level 3 evaluations seek to discover whether learning initiatives and programs actually made any difference by asking these questions: "What impact is the learning having? How well are learners applying what they learned?"

There are two primary methods for this level of assessment:

- Direct observation of performance or the results of performance

- Surveys and interviews with people who interact with learners or are affected by the results of their work

Level 3 evaluations can be performed only after people have had sufficient time to apply the learning. Collecting the necessary information requires such time-intensive activities as direct observation of learners while they are engaged in work activities; analyses of the results of learners' performance; or interviews with, or detailed surveys of, supervisors, colleagues, customers, and others.

Level 3 evaluations are time-consuming and costly to conduct, so organizations are often reluctant to invest the time or resources to conduct them. Yet this level of evaluation is very important: After all, what's the point of supporting organizational learning if it has no useful impact?

But what if you determine that a learning program is making no meaningful difference? Perhaps the learners simply haven't bothered to use what they learned or are actively resisting change. But you might be arriving at that conclusion too quickly. There can be many reasons why learning fails to make an impact, including these:

People have had little or no opportunity to apply the learning. For learning to stick, people need to use it right away. Otherwise, it is likely to be lost. Managers need to make sure that employees have opportunities to apply the learning on the job.

They do not have enough time. It takes longer to do something new or do something in a new way. The pressure to get things done quickly can make it difficult or impossible to use the new learning. For learning to effect change, learners may need extra time to experiment and practice.

They do not have the necessary equipment, resources, or information. In some cases, people do not have access to what they need in order to use the new learning on the job, such as the right technology, a database, or a client list. Without that access, they are unable to apply the learning. Managers need to make sure that employees have what they need.

The learning is no longer (or never was) relevant. The learning objectives may never have been linked to the organization's strategic goals or to the learner's performance or development goals. Changes in organizational policies or procedures may have made the learning irrelevant or unnecessary. The implementation of new systems, an organizational restructuring, or a reassignment might mean that the person no longer needs the learning. Level 3 evaluations help you spot these issues and take steps to ensure that learning programs are relevant to the organization and the individual employees.

Level 4. Results (Has the Learning Helped Us Achieve Our Goals?)

Top-performing organizations align learning with their business goals. Level 4 evaluations ask, "To what degree has our learning plan helped us achieve our goals?"

Level 4 evaluations require the collection of a great deal of information and the expertise to determine what it means. Organizations achieve or fail to achieve their goals for many reasons, only some of which can be linked to their learning plans. Improvements in safety might be due, at least in part, to a warehouse redesign; reduced profitability might be caused by economic conditions or unexpected expenses. To complicate matters, there is a seldom a clear baseline to use for comparison.

You may decide to skip Level 4 evaluations or limit them to the most important learning initiatives. When making that decision, however, keep in mind that this level of evaluation provides vital data that you need to determine whether your valuable resources are being put to the best use.

Level 5. Return on Investment (Is the Investment Worth the Cost?)

Successful organizations stay that way by examining the costs versus the benefits of everything they do. This final level of evaluation seeks to answer the question, "What is the ROI of our learning plan?"

Dr. Jack Phillips added this level of evaluation to Dr. Kirkpatrick's original model to address an issue that has become increasingly important: the need to examine the impact of every activity on business results. But as every CEO and business owner knows, determining ROI is a complex process. That's especially true when it comes to the ROI of learning.

Performing a Level 5 evaluation requires calculating all the costs of planning, designing, delivering, and following up your learning programs. Those costs include salaries and benefits of employees who are involved at any stage; consultant and instructor fees; program design or purchase; and technology, equipment, materials, and supplies. They also include the learners' time, both to learn and to practice applying the learning. For those reasons, most organizations limit Level 5 evaluations to the most important and most expensive programs.

> **To Consider:** What methods do you use to assess the success of your learning initiatives? How well are those methods working? What other methods might you need to use?
>
> **What's Next:** Learning plans have many moving parts. In Chapter 8, we'll explain how managing your learning operations helps you ensure that programs align with your mission, vision, and business needs; everything runs smoothly; you can easily see what's working and what's not; and you can respond quickly to change.

8

Managing Your Organization's Learning Operation

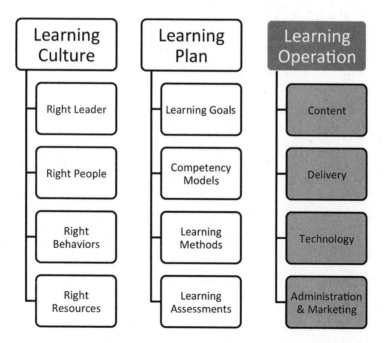

Sarder Framework: Building the Learning Organization

You've got to eat while you dream. You've got to deliver on short-range commitments, while you develop a long-range strategy and vision and implement it . . . walking and chewing gum if you will. Getting it done in the short-range, and delivering a long-range plan, and executing on that.[1]

—*Jack Welch*

M anaging your learning plans is a little like managing a family. Every day brings innumerable things that need to be done—get the kids off to school and yourself off to work, keep the refrigerator stocked, plan and prepare meals, do the laundry, oversee the homework, pay the bills . . . and then there's getting Jennie to soccer and Sam to his piano lesson, taking the car in to see why it keeps stalling, finding a sitter for Saturday night, meeting with the kids' teachers, planning a vacation . . . the tasks seem endless. It takes careful management and attention to detail to make sure everything gets done, done on time, and done right. It's hard to do unless you have a system.

Developing and carrying out an organization-wide learning plan requires an even larger number of tasks and involves large numbers of people. It also involves enormous amounts of information and a great deal of technology. Without attentive oversight and effective systems, your learning operation can quickly become fragmented, redundant, inefficient, and disconnected from the organization's mission, values, business needs, and strategic goals. When that happens, even the best learning plan will be unlikely to achieve meaningful results, no matter how many resources you allot for learning programs and activities.

A comprehensive system for managing your learning operation is essential for you to be able to:

- Avoid unnecessary redundancy and control costs

- Align learning initiatives, team and individual learning plans, and learning activities throughout the organization, and determine how well they are achieving the desired outcomes

- Keep competency models up to date as your business changes

- Project your future learning and development needs

- Develop, customize, update, reuse, and improve learning content

- Streamline administrative tasks, such as scheduling courses, registering participants, and tracking completion rates

- Organize and store course content and materials, assessment results, participant data, and vendors and instructor information

- Integrate learning into HR initiatives, such as performance management, career development, compensation planning, and succession planning

- Demonstrate compliance with government and industry-specific certification requirements

- Respond quickly to change and identify ways to improve your learning plan

The Components of a Learning Operation

Although the boundaries are not always clearly delineated, the work needed to manage your learning operation can be categorized into four broad functions.

Content

Content forms the heart of your learning operation. Organizational learning involves an enormous amount of content, including curricula and course materials, assessments, tests, competency models, employee performance and development plans, employee evaluations, and more. To keep your learning operation running smoothly and avoid wasting resources, all that content needs to be organized and managed so that it is easy to access and easy to update.

Delivery

It wasn't all that long ago that the bulk of an organization's learning budget went to the design or purchase of classroom programs, where people learned together in a group. As we discussed in Chapter 6, the classroom is migrating to the Web: Virtual workshops and seminars make it possible for people to learn in a group no matter where in the world they are. In addition, learning is increasingly being delivered in a variety of digital forms, such as e-learning, video, webcast, podcast, and massive open online courses (MOOCs), reducing costs and expanding the reach of your learning initiatives by making learning available to employees whenever and wherever they need it.

Technology

Within only a few generations, technology has revolutionized the way we work. It's almost impossible to imagine how we would manage today's complex learning operations without it, so it goes without saying that the right technologies used in the right way are essential tools for managing your learning plan.

The benefits of learning system technologies go well beyond streamlining administrative tasks, storing curriculum, and delivering e-learning programs. Today's sophisticated technologies increase collaboration by enabling the efficient sharing of knowledge throughout the organization. They encourage and facilitate learning by making learning programs of all kinds readily available to everyone who needs them and include reporting functions that provide the data you need to evaluate your learning plan and identify ways to improve it. When integrated with your HR systems, they help maintain all the content related to your employees' performance and development, which helps you identify competency gaps and development needs and find the most cost-effective ways to address them.

An increasing number of vendors offer an increasingly complex array of technologies. At the end of this chapter, you'll find an overview of the options and tips for determining what technologies are best for your organization.

Administration and Marketing

The administrative and marketing function helps you make sure that all the tasks involved in managing a learning operation get done, done right, and done in the most cost-effective way. You need to set up a system and processes for handling that function, which typically does the following:

Manage the process of developing, purchasing, and customizing courses and learning programs. Few organizations have sufficient in-house resources to provide all the learning programs employees need. Even if you do have skilled instructional designers on staff, you are likely to find it cost-effective to bring in consultants to design and conduct certain learning programs, purchase off-the-shelf programs, and send employees to public classes, workshops, and seminars.

Maintain a searchable inventory of learning-related content. Content that cannot be easily accessed is of little use. People need to be able to find the right course or program to meet a specific need, the right instructors and vendors for a specific learning activity, or learning assessments—anything they need to achieve their learning goals. A good content management system that makes it easy to find specific content increases efficiency and improves learning outcomes.

Locate and select the right suppliers, vendors, and instructors, and set up a searchable database. Learning is big business, with private companies, universities, and consultants offering a vast range of programs and services. To achieve your learning goals, you need to sort through the innumerable options to identify the right public courses, instructional designers, facilitators, presenters, instructors, and technology systems; negotiate pricing, terms, and conditions; and prepare contracts. Storing that information in a form that managers and employees can easily access helps avoid reinventing the wheel every time a new need emerges.

Manage your tuition assistance programs. According to the National Bureau of Economic Research (NBER), surveys by Hewett Associates (1993) and the Society for Human Resources (2002) found that 79 to 99 percent of organizations studied offered tuition assistance. The NBER also reported an American Council of Education estimate that 20 percent of graduate students and 6 percent of undergraduates receive some financial support from their employers.[2] In 2011, the National Association of Colleges and Employers Student Survey found that tuition reimbursement is the third most desirable employee benefit, behind 100 percent employer-paid medical coverage and salary increases.[3]

Helping employees further their education is an investment that makes good sense. Well-educated employees are better able to contribute to the organization's success; if they are given the chance to use the learning, they are more likely to stay.

Tuition assistance is an expensive benefit, however. At this time, few organizations—Google among them—offer tuition assistance to all full-time employees, and Starbucks is one of the only companies that provides financial support for part-timers to attend college. Many organizations pay only for courses that are directly linked to an employee's job or internal career path. Nearly all restrict tuition reimbursement to employees who have been with the organization for

(continued)

(continued)

a specific amount of time or are at certain levels. Although some pay educational institutions directly, most provide support in the form of reimbursement after a course or program has been completed, so employees must first come up with tuition payments themselves. Employees may also need to maintain certain grades to qualify.

Like the rest of your learning plan, tuition assistance programs need to be carefully managed and monitored to determine how well they are working: How many employees are participating? What courses are they taking? What impact is their education having on their ability to contribute to the organization's success? How long are they remaining with the organization after completing a program or receiving a degree? What's the actual return on your investment?

Market and promote your learning initiatives and programs. Top learning organizations continuously promote the value of learning and encourage ongoing learning at every level. An important function of your learning operation will be to keep learning at the forefront of people's minds, incorporate learning into everyday activities, promote your learning programs, and find ways to increase employees' motivation to participate in learning activities.

Marketing Tips

- Hold presentations and discussions at the organization and team levels about what a learning organization is, how learning relates to success, and what the organization is doing or plans to do to become a learning organization.

- Publish a newsletter or internal blog with learning-related stories and tips and celebrations of learning success.

- Post flyers in prominent places throughout the organization and on online bulletin boards to announce learning initiatives and remind people of the importance of learning.

- Use chat, e-mail, and other electronic communication methods to announce and publicize classes and other learning opportunities.

Analyze data and prepare reports. An effective system for managing your learning operation collects and analyzes the data you need to assess the success of your learning initiatives and measure the return on your investment. The reports the system generates will help you and your team determine what's working, what's not, and what needs to be changed.

The Role of a Chief Learning Officer (CLO)

In the early 1990s, GE CEO Jack Welch created the position of chief learning officer and named Steve Kerr the company's first CLO. Before that time, the responsibility for an organization's learning and development activities typically resided in the HR, training and development, or organizational development offices. That is still the case in many organizations. But today's top organizations are increasingly centralizing the responsibility for learning in the hands of senior corporate officers and their teams, decision makers with the ability to influence others. The job title is not always chief learning officer, but the job is essentially the same: Determine how to best carry out the organization's learning plan and help the organization keep getting better.

A CLO typically is responsible for the following:

- Building and maintaining a learning culture and communicating the value of learning throughout the organization

- Developing leaders who support and encourage ongoing learning and serve as role models for their employees

- Working with senior management and others to develop the organization's learning plan and integrate it with the organization's HR initiatives

- Ensuring that learning plans and initiatives align with the organization's values, mission, and strategic goals and that learning initiatives focus on the critical competencies the organization needs to succeed

- Assessing the outcomes of learning initiatives to determine whether they are meeting goals, making the best use of resources, and providing a sufficient return on the organization's investment

- Facilitating and overseeing communication between senior management, HR and learning and development staff, managers, and others

- Ensuring that the organization has effective systems, processes, and technology in place to keep the organization's learning operation running smoothly and efficiently

The Role of a Learning Management Service

Developing and implementing your learning plan is too important and too complex to go it alone. A learning management service that has access to validated competency models and assessment instruments, up-to-the minute sourcing databases, the latest technological tools, and expertise in the field of learning can guide you through the process, provide advice and recommendations, and handle many tasks more efficiently than you could on your own. This service can also work with you to sort through the many product options, many of which are very costly, to help you avoid an all-too-common mistake—purchasing a Tesla when a Prius would do.

A good learning management service can help you and your team:

- Assess the current state of affairs, identify learning goals, and develop competency models based on your mission, values, goals, and business needs

- Develop your learning plan, implement your learning initiatives, manage your learning operation, and assess the outcomes

- Identify employees' performance gaps and development needs and determine the most cost-effective ways to meet them

- Identify and evaluate sourcing options

- Measure learning outcomes and recommend necessary changes to make your learning plan more effective and efficient

- Keep abreast of the latest research, products, and trends in learning

Choosing the Right Technologies

Choosing the best learning system technologies depends on factors that include your in-house capabilities and the complexity of your learning operation. The decision can be complicated by the fact that the terminology used to refer to those technologies is used inconsistently, with a great deal of overlap. How do you know whether you need an LMS, an EPPS, a LCMS, or a CMS? It's enough to make your head spin. Here's a quick primer.

Learning management system (LMS). The American Society for Training & Development (ASTD) defines an LMS as "a software application that automates the administration, tracking, and reporting of training events."[4] Originally designed for the classroom and adopted by businesses primarily to deliver and manage e-learning, the LMS market is now $2.6 billion and is poised to reach $7.83 billion by 2018.[5] Today's products include far broader functions, which typically include course scheduling and registration tasks; tracking course completion rates; analyzing competency gaps and creating learning paths; tracking learners' progress; issuing certifications; storing content; maintaining vendor, instructor, and consultant databases; and issuing reports. In fact, the term LMS is now commonly used interchangeably with the other terms that describe automated systems for managing learning initiatives.

Learning content management system (LCMS). The first LCMSs were designed to allow course developers to create, store, revise, reuse, and deliver digital learning content; create personalized learning paths; and track learners' progress. Today, products referred to as "LCMS" are likely to incorporate all or most of the functions of an LMS.

Content management system (CMS). Essentially, a CMS is what it says it is: a system for managing the content and delivery of learning programs. A CMS stores course materials online, tracks learners' performance, and facilitates communication between the instructors and learners. Most of today's sophisticated LMSs incorporate CMS functions.

Electronic performance support system (EPPS). In the 1990s, performance specialist Gloria Gery defined an EPPS as "an integrated electronic environment that is available to and easily accessible by each employee and is structured to provide immediate, individualized on-line access to the full range of information, software, guidance, advice and assistance, data, images, tools, and assessment and monitoring systems to permit job performance with minimal support and intervention by others."[6] In other words, an EPPS is an electronic form of a time-honored tool, the job aid, which helps people learn in real time, while they are actually carrying out job-related tasks.

Talent management system (TMS). This term refers to software used to manage what are often called the four pillars of HR management: recruitment, performance, learning and development, and compensation management. A typical TMS helps you identify quality applicants for a position, track employee goals and progress, provide employees with learning opportunities, and link compensation to performance. Ideally, your TMS will include or be fully integrated with your LMS.

Software as a service (SaaS). Sometimes called "on-demand" software, SaaS usually refers to software that is licensed on a subscription basis and accessed via a Web browser, instead of being purchased and installed on the user's computer. One advantage is that the software can be easily updated.

Shareable content object reference model (SCORM). A SCORM is a collection of standards for authoring content in an LMS so that the content can be shared between systems.

Computer learning content information management system (CLCIMS). This term refers to any SCORM-compliant LMS or LCMS.

Tips for Deciding What Technology You Need

If you were planning to hold a big event, perhaps a family reunion or corporate retreat, you would need to look for a place that met specific requirements: large enough for your group, the right location, available at the right time, the right cost, and, of course, the right food. You also have certain requirements when you shop for technology. Here are some of the questions to ask.

What do you need the technology to do? This is the first question when selecting any technology, from cell phones to software. Think about what you'll need it to do, how and when you'll use it, and what other systems it will interface with.

How extensive is your IT capability? What can you do yourself, and what do you need outside help to do? Do you have the in-house expertise to develop or customize the necessary technology, or do you need products that are ready to go and easy to learn? Would it be more cost-effective to work with experts who have the expertise and knowledge to help you select, set up, and manage the right systems than to do it on your own?

Do you have an automated HR system? If so, look for management technology that is compatible with, and can be synchronized with, your existing system.

Do you need technology that supports third-party courseware? Some learning management technology is compatible only with the vendor's own products. For more flexibility, choose technology that supports a wide range of products.

What's your budget? Technology can take a huge bite out of an organization's budget. Determine how much you can afford to spend, and do a cost-benefit analysis. In some cases, you might find that spending more up front can save significant costs down the line.

To Consider: As you implement your organization-wide learning plan, what are some steps you can take to manage it efficiently? Are you already using any learning-related technology? How well is it working? What other or different technology might you need?

What's Next: In centuries past, people could succeed at a job or in a profession with a focused, limited set of skills and knowledge. But today's workers need more. Today, the ability to succeed and thrive depends increasingly not on what people know but on how well they are able to learn. That's what we'll explore in the final chapter of this book.

9

Call to Action!

Vice President Zhang Jiyong of Beijing Open University recently held a graduation ceremony for 94-year-old Lu Juzhong. In her graduation speech, she said that learning brought vitality to her old life and made it possible for her to broaden her horizons. Although life may be limited, the acquisition of knowledge is an endless process, she said, adding that "she would set up a new learning plan and apply herself to the gaining of new knowledge throughout her life."[1]

—Yu Zhiwen

What's amazing is, if young people understood how doing well in school makes the rest of their life so much [more] interesting, they would be more motivated. It's so far away in time that they can't appreciate what it means for their whole life.[2]

—Bill Gates

A December 2014 *New York Times* article reported that "even with the economy's recent improvement, the share of working-age adults who are working is substantially lower than a decade ago—and lower than any point in the 1990s."[3] The same month, the Kaiser Family Foundation reported the findings from a *New York Times*/Kaiser Foundation/CBS News poll: "While the official U.S. unemployment rate has declined since the start of the recession in late 2007, the total share of adults who are not employed has risen in recent years."[4]

Why is that happening?

One reason is that work itself is changing. It has been changing for quite a while now, but like everything else today, the changes are becoming increasingly rapid. Many of the jobs for which people prepared themselves no longer exist or require competencies they do not have. Technology is transforming every aspect of the workplace. Robots, which have been assembling cars and doing clerical work for years now, are becoming more capable by the day, and the latest word is that artificial intelligence is starting to replace humans in certain knowledge and service jobs.[5] Where it will all lead is the subject of concerned debate in every sector.

There is only one skill that we know people will need as old jobs are replaced with new and different jobs, and that is a skill that too many, sadly, lack: the ability to learn. Learners have the advantage when things change. Instead of holding fast to outdated skills and concepts, they embrace the opportunity to expand what they know and are able to do. They don't hold themselves back because they fear failing or being seen as lacking knowledge. Instead, their attitude toward change is "Great, bring it on!"

Become an Activist in the Service of Learning

Develop a passion for learning. If you do, you'll never cease to grow.[6]

—*Anthony J. D'Angelo*

I think lifelong learning is important for society because of the example we set for the next generation. If we want to sustain our way of life and we want to make sure that people have lives that are valuable and in balance, we have to get better at that. Potentially, we will be happier too. Statistics show that people who love what they do are healthier and have less stress in their lives. Those people are learning. Those people are lifelong learners.[7]

—*Laurie Carey*

I wrote this book because I care about learning and passionately believe that learning is the key not only to career success but also to health and happiness. I think that this is a particularly crucial time to promote learning so that we, our children, our colleagues and our employees—everyone—can keep up with change and make the most of the advances in technology that for the first time in history have put all the knowledge of the world at our fingertips. We can work together to make our world a better place by becoming activists who create learning organizations in the service of learning, become lifelong learners ourselves, and strive to improve education and learning opportunities for everyone.

Action 1. Build a Learning Organization

A learning journey is a people journey. It is both a continuous "search for the truth" and an emotional journey. One of your roles as a leader or manager or teammate is to "invite, include, and inspire" others to join you in the learning journey.[8]

—*Edward D. Hess*

We've talked throughout this book about why becoming a learning organization is vital to your organization's success. But there's more to it than success. Building a learning organization is a key action in support of learning.

Learning organizations spread learning around, to their employees, their customers, their suppliers—all the people with whom they interact. That's because they do things differently. Instead of providing pat answers to questions, they encourage people to find the answers themselves. Rather than telling people how to solve problems, they help them come up with solutions themselves. Instead of rejecting new ideas and new ways of doing things, they encourage and support experimentation. In learning organizations, leaders openly share information, ask for help, admit mistakes, and acknowledge the limitations of their knowledge. Those are all learning behaviors. And when people work in an environment that promotes learning, they are more likely to become learners themselves and to promote learning to others.

Action 2. Become a Lifelong Learner

In our knowledge economy, if you haven't learned how to learn, you'll have a hard time.[9]

—*Peter Drucker*

The beautiful thing about learning is that no one can take it away from you.[10]

—*B. B. King*

A few years ago my dad asked me, "Russell, did you know that when you were five years old, you could recite the names and capital cities of all 192 countries?"

I was shocked to find this out because I can no longer remember those names and had no idea that I had ever had that knowledge. The conversation reminded me that the human brain is like a bucket with holes in it. As we learn new things, we fill the bucket, but it is constantly leaking. Think about it: Do you remember everything you learned in high school or college?

We need to learn new things daily to keep the bucket full. Like Lu Juzhong, we need to be lifelong learners. A passion for learning, as I discovered after years of research and reading, is one of the key characteristics of all successful people.

But lifelong learning offers more than increased opportunities to move up in the world and make enough money to live the kind of life you want. Houses can be foreclosed on, gold rises and falls in value, but no one can take away the value of knowledge. Learning enriches your life.

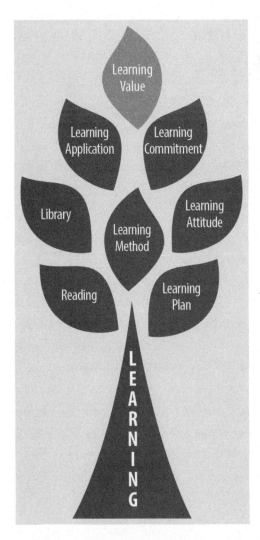

The Learning Tree

As I said in the introduction of my first book, *Learning: Steps to Becoming a Passionate Lifelong Learner*, and in this book as well, love of learning has dominated both my career as CEO of Netcom Learning and my personal life. I wrote my books to help inspire others to become lifelong learners, and I hope these steps will inspire you.

Appreciate the value of attaining continuous knowledge. Learning can benefit you in so many ways. I had an employee who had been a successful lawyer. But he had gone into law to please his parents, and in midlife he decided to change careers to something he felt passionate about: teaching and information technology. He took courses, read everything he could get his hands on, took on an internship, and became certified in the areas in which he wanted to teach. He ended up being one of our best trainers, recognized by Microsoft for his expertise—and making more money at his chosen career than he had ever made as a lawyer.

Embrace being a committed lifelong learner. So many of us have the desire to change our lives and careers, but without commitment, those dreams can float away like balloons at a child's birthday party. Commitment creates the difference between wishing for something and attaining it. Like my employee, once you find your passion and commit to it, there will be no stopping you—you cannot learn enough.

Develop the right attitude toward continuous learning. I believe there are three types of learners. The *don't care* learner has little curiosity; the status quo is perfectly fine with her. She prefers passive activities, such as watching television and playing

computer games; dislikes reading; and will attend learning programs only when forced by a job requirement. Even then she
drags her feet, fidgets, sighs, and checks her phone; she is
physically present but mentally far way.

The *know it all* learner believes he knows everything and
doesn't need to learn anything more. He's the first to declare his
expertise, even when he has only rudimentary knowledge. Of all
learners, he knows the least because he has stopped growing.

Then there is the *don't know enough* learner. She is actively
learning throughout her life and always has a book by her side, a
goal in her mind, and a new idea she is considering. This learner
seems more alive, because she is open to all topics and interested
in whatever new knowledge she encounters. She knows that
embracing the infinite possibilities of knowledge is the key to
her success and embracing a pro-learning attitude makes all the
difference in what she makes of her life.

Develop an effective learning plan to excel in your field.   Just as
you need a learning plan for your organization to succeed, you
need a learning plan for yourself. Throughout my career, I've
benefited from a learning plan that included the *learning goals* I
hoped to achieve, the *competencies* I wanted to master, the *learning
methods* for attaining new skills, and *learning assessments* for
measuring my progress and determining what adjustments to
make to my plan. As I discovered, the beauty of a learning plan is
that it can be changed as your career and business evolve.

**Become an effective learner by combining a variety of learning
methods.**   The Internet has given us a treasure that our grand-
parents could never have imagined: free, easy access to the world's
accumulated knowledge and ideas. With TED Talks; free online
courses; YouTube videos; free or reasonably priced university

classes; and far, far more available on every subject imaginable, we have no excuse not to be lifelong learners. Use that access to enrich your life by seeking opportunities to learn something new: a language, a musical instrument, how to play tennis or become a better manager, history or philosophy, new technology, teaching—whatever interests you, challenges you, and broadens your horizons.

Also, think about how you prefer to learn—by reading? Self-study? In a classroom? On the job? Working with a mentor or a coach? You'll get more enjoyment out of learning and the learning will be more effective if you understand how to mix and match the methods that work best for you to learn different things in different situations.

Read an hour each day.

> Have you ever watched a child who is learning to read? The way she concentrates so completely that her tongue sticks out or her toes curl. The way she persists. And then, her sheer joy as she recognizes the letters, spells a word, reads a sentence, and, finally reads a whole book. . . . That joy is there for all of us when we push ourselves to the limit and slightly beyond.[11]
> —*Douglas Conant and Mette Norgaard*

As with many people, my most influential role model was my father. When I was a boy in Bangladesh, he would return home from a long day as the director of a local hospital, not to sit in front of the television, but to read late into the night. It's not surprising that I caught his passion for reading. If you read biographies of successful people, you will discover that they are all avid readers. As Bill Gates says, "If you want to do something good for children, the most important thing you can do is cultivate a love of reading."[12]

Unfortunately, we are not a nation of readers—far from it. In 2013, a YouGov/*Huffington Post* poll found that more than 25 percent of the people polled had not read a print book or an e-book book during the previous year.[13] Pew Research Center studies in 2012 had similar results: One-quarter of our population does not read books, and among those who do read, only a small percentage read more than a handful of books a year.[14]

Those statistics are surprising when you notice that very young children love books. Toddlers love being read to, love trying to learn the words, carry their books around, and sit happily paging through them again and again. Yet, by the time they've completed a grade or two in school, too many children find reading a chore instead of a joy. Reading becomes just another assignment: Read a certain number of assigned paragraphs or for a certain amount of time and write a report or take a quiz. No wonder kids lose interest, turning instead to the YouTube videos and computer games that capture their attention.

There's no easy answer. Educators, parents, and others continually struggle to find ways to help children become more motivated to read, and there is a great deal of controversy about how to do it. But one thing is clear: Reading is fundamental to learning. If we want our children to become lifelong learners, we have to find a way.

Build your own library.   When I grew up in Bangladesh, reading and learning were favored endeavors for children, the equivalent of playing sports for an American boy. I loved to read and essentially grew up in the library of the hospital where my father was the director. It was a library my father had helped build for the hospital's employees and their children. In those early years, I mostly read textbooks and memorized Bengali poetry. The beauty and lyricism of these poems have remained with me for more than 30 years.

Libraries are vast repositories of knowledge that teaches, inspires, and makes life meaningful. A library of your own, whether physical or electronic, gives you a personal collection of knowledge you can access whenever you want. Your library keeps you learning.

Apply what you have learned.   There is little point in developing a learning plan if you end up ignoring it, and a book does you no good if it gathers dust by your bed. For learning to unleash its power, you need to apply it, consistently and with dedication. A well-known quote that has long been misattributed to the poet Goethe is worth remembering: "Whatever you can do or dream you can, begin it. Boldness has genius, power, and magic in it!"[15] Find out what you're good at and what you're passionate about, keep learning, and apply what you learn to keep getting better in your work and in your life.

Action 3. Promote Lifelong Learning

You must be the change you wish to see in the world.[16]
                                        —*Mahatma Gandhi*

Education is the most powerful weapon which you can use to change the world.[17]
                                        —*Nelson Mandela*

Change will not come if we wait for some other person or if we wait for some other time. We are the ones we've been waiting for. We are the change that we seek.[18]
                                        —*Barack Obama*

Change starts with us. By continuously demonstrating our own commitment to learning, we can be role models for others. By continuously promoting lifelong learning, we can effect real change in attitudes, behaviors, laws, and processes.

Talk about the value of learning every chance you get. Promote a culture of learning in your family, your organization, and your community; at the dinner table; in meetings; and with groups. Encourage discussions about books, movies, and current events. Ask questions of family members, friends, colleagues, and others to help them learn from problems, make informed decisions, and figure out how to make things better. Share stories that illustrate what learning means to you.

Be an Education Activist

The education system is failing our children. It is not designed for the way that we operate today. With smartphones at our fingertips, we really don't have to remember anything, so the drive to keep on filling their heads with lots of information is pointless. Our young people are not being taught how to figure things out, how to solve problems. That's a major challenge. We have to be willing to stop and say what we're doing right now is not working. We need to make a change.[19]

—Jill Johnson

You can teach a student a lesson for a day; but if you can teach him to learn by creating curiosity, he will continue the learning process as long as he lives.[20]

—Clay P. Bedford

In his book, *Learn or Die*, Dr. Edward D. Hess writes, "The current consensus is that a good educational learning environment is one that fosters intrinsic motivation and gives students some autonomy and control over their learning . . . where there are good role models (teachers) for learning and creativity, and where the style of teaching meets the diverse needs of learners . . . the learning process resembles a journey of discovery . . . learners experience a combination of positive support and positive challenges."[21]

Does that statement describe the U.S. education system? Sadly, most people would say no.

Yet we are born with enthusiasm for learning and a great capacity to learn. Young children are constantly experimenting, getting things wrong, learning from their mistakes, and trying again and again until they get it right. Successful learners carry that enthusiasm beyond childhood. Curious and excited by the challenge of learning something new, they actively seek learning opportunities.

But too many of our schoolchildren find learning a chore. Their natural curiosity, instead of being nurtured, is dampened or snuffed out entirely. For them, learning is an endless routine of memorizing facts and taking tests. Rather than being an exciting place that encourages discovery, school is boring and seemingly not relevant to their lives. The failure of so many of our schools to keep students interested and motivated shows in our dismal success rate: Even though we rank near the top in per-pupil spending on education, we rank twenty-first in the world when it comes to high school graduation.[22]

It's not that we don't know that we must get better at engaging our students in learning; we do. What we don't know is how best to go about it. Theories abound and are endlessly argued, with little action. Successful pilot programs that could point the way are ignored. In part because we have no centralized system for managing our schools or making decisions about what and how to teach, we engage in ongoing controversies between federal and state governments, school boards, parents, teachers, and educators about the best way to educate our kids: testing/no testing, Common Core/no Common Core, online learning/traditional classroom learning. What's lost in these sometimes heated discussions is the kids themselves: how to engage them in learning and help them develop the competencies they need to be productive, successful members of our society.

Partnership for 21st Century Learning (P21), which seeks to "serve as a catalyst to position 21st century readiness at the center of United States' K12 education by building collaborative partnerships among education, business, community and government leaders,"[23] is one of many organizations advocating changes in our educational system. P21 members believe that there is a "profound gap between the knowledge and skills most students learn in school and the knowledge and skills they need in typical 21st century communities and workplaces."[24] In a letter to Congress on June 2, 2014, P21 stated: "Studies show that far too many students leave school unprepared for the next stage of their lives, lacking the full breadth of knowledge *and* skills for higher education or work."[25]

P21 members believe that today's students, in addition to becoming proficient in reading and writing, math and science, languages, civics, economics, the arts, history, and geography, need other essential competencies: critical thinking, problem solving, communication, collaboration, creativity, and innovation.

What can *we* do to make that happen?

We can help make it happen by advocating action and taking action ourselves. That's what organizations such as P21 are trying to do, but they can't do it alone. Our education system will not change unless we as a society drive that change. Each and every one of us, parent or not, business owner or not, needs to encourage, support, and promote learning for everyone, at all ages and all levels of society.

Speak loudly and often about the need to engage our children in learning, and teach them what they need for success in the twenty-first century. Support advocacy groups. Attend school board meetings—or run for the school board yourself. Support legislators who make improving education a priority. Speak out for changes in higher education to provide equal access for all students, make college affordable, and redesign college and university curricula to focus on the competencies that today's students need to attain.

Together, we can make the difference.

"The classroom of the future probably won't be led by a robot with arms and legs, but it may be guided by a digital brain," reported William Huntsberry on NPR in January 2015, describing his visit to the sixth-grade math class at David Boody Junior High School in Brooklyn, New York, where computer algorithms like the ones used for Google searches guide students' activities.[26] A computer makes the daily individualized assignments and administers a short test to measure what the student learned that day.

The program, called Teach to One, has had mixed results. A Harvard researcher, Justin Reich, believes that it could be effective but has yet to have more than moderate results. Critics say that although algorithms can streamline certain mechanized tasks and administer standardized tests, their overuse can detract from helping students attain essential competencies, such as creativity and critical thinking.

In his book *The End of College*, Professor Kevin Carey, director of the Education Policy Program at the New America Foundation, explains that at the University of Everywhere, "educational resources that have been scarce and expensive for centuries will be abundant and free." According to Carey, our current system of higher education is not a "system of opportunity [but] a system of replicating privilege that already exists." In the future, he believes, learning will be open to everyone, regardless of economic status, and "the idea of 'admission' to college will become an anachronism, because the University of Everywhere will be open to everyone."[27]

To Consider: What steps will you take to use what you have learned in this book in order to help your organization succeed by creating a learning culture and implementing a learning plan? What will you do to become a lifelong learner and to promote the value of learning in your family, your community, your country, and the world?

Learning from Experts

Excerpts from Sarder TV Interviews

One of the best ways to learn is from other people. Since 2012, our Sarder TV business has asked more than 100 organizational leaders, authors, educators, and learning and development experts to share their learning with us. Below are excerpts from a few of those interviews. For complete versions of all the interviews we've conducted, visit www.sardertv.com.

Authors and Educators

Peter Senge

Author of the widely acclaimed book *The Fifth Discipline: The Art & Practice of the Learning Organization* (1990) and numerous other publications, Peter Senge is a senior lecturer in leadership and sustainability at the Massachusetts Institute of Technology Sloan School of Management. Senge is one of the 24 people who has had the greatest influence on business strategy over the last 100 years, according to the *Journal of Business Strategy*, and he has been named one of the world's top management gurus by the *Financial Times* and *BusinessWeek*.

Senge has lectured extensively throughout the world, translating the abstract ideas of systems theory into tools for better understanding of economic and organizational change. His work articulates a cornerstone position of human values in the workplace, namely, that vision, purpose, reflectiveness, and systems thinking are essential if organizations are to realize their potential. Senge is the founding chair of the Society for Organizational Learning North America (SoL), a global community of corporations, researchers, and consultants dedicated to the "interdependent development of people and their institutions,"[1] and cofounder of the Academy for Systemic Change, which seeks to accelerate the growth of the field of systemic change worldwide.

There's a fascinating concept in your book in which you say our actions can actually create reality. Tell us more about it and how it can inform organizational management.

I've always thought the most eloquent definition of systems thinking is seeing how our actions shape our reality. When our oldest son was three or four [he'd come back from the playground and say] "So, so, and so's a good friend." A month later, that friend would be somebody he didn't like at all: "Oh, he's really a jerk." Every kid has this story, right? But if you examine it, you'll often see something like this: "We were playing and he threw sand in my face." "Now why did he throw the sand in your face?" "Yesterday he asked to use my truck and I told him no, so he got really mad." The basic problem here is the child doesn't see that getting sand in his face today was a result of being unwilling to share his truck yesterday. He doesn't see what in engineering we used to call the feedback loop between something I did and its later consequence. Not seeing this delayed effect of his actions, he then reacts to the consequences as if they had nothing to do with him. For most of us, such incidents signal the roots of lifelong struggle. We don't see the many ramifications of what we do on others around us, so their actions or reactions are obtuse to us.

[In the same way] Businesses don't see the consequences of their actions on the communities in which they operate, and societies don't see the consequences of their actions on other societies. They don't see how following their self-interest caused problems for others. So whether it's on a playground or on the global stage, this inability to see the larger system leads us to not seeing how we are, in fact, shaping our reality.

Part of your update of *The Fifth Discipline* was to include reflections from practice in the years that have gone by since it first came out in 1990. What is one reflection from practice that stands out for you?

First off, it was a lot of fun because I picked people I really wanted to talk to, a small set of my own heroes, people I admired enormously. Getting on the phone with them for an hour and then writing something and then sending it back to them—it was a great pleasure.

One was Dame Barbara Stocking, who was the president of Oxfam (originally Oxford Famine Relief). In Europe, it's probably the single most well-known social justice (nongovernmental organization) NGO. There are about 20 Oxfams all around the world. Barbara was the president for about 10 years. She was remarkably effective. I will never forget that she made a simple comment which illuminated a lot. She said, "You know, I've always been a developmentally oriented manager. The development of my people has always been as important to me as producing results. I've always seen those two as connected." That was a very simple articulation. I'd never heard the cornerstone of the work we'd all been involved in [described that directly].

What are the three core learning capabilities?

This took many years and we had a lot of different kinds of ideas, but gradually it coalesced into one: the spirit of deep intention, or aspiration. At some point the learner crystallizes a vision—something they really want to be able to do. Without that, the learning process never happens. Building the capability to foster that vision personally and collectively has always been a core leadership capability.

But, then you try things and they don't work. So the ability to reflect is equally central to learning: "We tried that; what happened?" It's hard to think of any learning process—walking, riding a bicycle, anything—that isn't a basic process of trying something and seeing how it works. But when you're learning to walk or learning to ride a bicycle, the reflection process is a little more immediate. In an organizational setting, that reflective dynamic is much more "complex"—the consequences of our actions are usually distant in time and space—and involves many, many people. If you look at how leading software companies work today, the best ones have people whose roles are to get people together and reflect. They gather a lot of data, but the data by itself usually doesn't tell them what they need to understand. The process of going from an observation to an understanding is a process of reflection. What did we expect to happen? What did happen? How do we have to think differently to get the outcome we want? That's the process of reflection, and in an organizational or work setting, it has to be collective in order to have an impact. That's the second core capacity. We've often called it the capacity for reflective conversation—to have a quality of conversation that allows people to actually enhance their ability to think and to think together effectively in complex settings.

The third capability is to understand the complexity, to see the larger system. This has always been a problem in businesses. Everybody gets fragmented. "You do this," "You do this," and

"You do this"—and everybody forgets what everybody else is doing because they're so busy doing their own thing. The assembly line is the archetypal example of fragmentation in work. Today, all organizations suffer from "silos," "stovepipes," "chimneys," "turf"—the different ways we verbally characterize fragmentation. Though the metaphors differ in different parts of the world or the country, the underlying problem is common: not seeing how it goes together. Not being able to step back and say, "Wait a second. If you do it this way, and you do this, and you do this, it actually might not add up to what we want." So helping people see the larger system is always a crucial leadership skill, today more than ever. This is why working in teams has become one of the most important developments in management in the past 20 to 30 years. In a team, different people have a little greater chance to put things together and think about what each one of them is doing. But doing this well takes skill and openness—that is why there is such a large variation in the effectiveness of teams. Plus, between the teams, people can still kind of get into a lot of trouble. But at least it has been a move in the right direction.

But, increasingly, the systems we need to understand do not just operate within individual organizations; they arise across networks of organizations, in industries and in geographic regions, and in some cases, like climate change, literally across the globe. For example, in the food industry, a small but growing number of leading companies are trying to see what it takes to manage the whole of a food supply chain, in order to insure the well-being of the farmers and the health of the farming ecology—in short, the viability of their business over the long term. If you don't manage the whole system, ultimately it will fail, and that's exactly what is happening in a lot of agriculture around the world today.

So those are the three core capabilities: cultivate aspiration, reflection, and seeing the larger system.

What are the first four disciplines of a learning organization?

I think [the original version of *The Fifth Discipline*] started off with personal mastery and building shared vision, and then mental models and team learning.

For example, everyone wants [their teams and organizations] to have shared visions. But shared visions don't grow from thin air. They are outgrowths of individual visions. If you don't create an environment where people can really think about what matters to them, you're not going to get a shared vision. In a sense, personal vision is the soil that shared visions can be grown in. If you don't have the right soil nutrients, forget it. It doesn't matter how hard you work, what you'll get is everybody saying, "Yes sir, boss. We've got the vision." But it doesn't mean anything. It's just a hollow expression of one or two or three people's goal, foisted on the organization. So you have to create an environment where people can be growing personally, developing their own sense of purpose and vision, their own capacities to accomplish the things they really want to accomplish. [But] it's very, very hard for organizations to embrace the idea that they're actually creating an environment for each person to grow.

Building shared vision is an outgrowth of personal mastery. At the personal level, what does it mean to cultivate my ability, or develop my ability to reflect? We all see the world as we see it and then we get mixed up and we think that, what we see is "that is." It's the fundamental error of all perception. "Oh yeah, I heard what she said." But if you actually go back and listen to a recording of what was said, it wasn't what was said at all—it's what I heard she said. We all hear what we hear and we take what we hear as the facts. So that gap between what actually happens and what we perceive to happen is the fundamental gap that requires reflection. We're not recording devices—none of us hears exactly what's said. None of us sees exactly what happened. In a nonreflective orientation, which is the common one, we take our awareness as fact.

That integrates into the fourth discipline of team learning because what creates a real learning environment in a team, at its most fundamental level, is a group of people who are willing to reflect and say, "Here's how I see it, but I know I don't see the whole picture. How do you see it?" Reflecting together is actually the core of team learning. So those are the first four disciplines.

In the book you talk about learning as "metanoia." Talk to us about that learning.

It was a word we used before we had the term "learning organization." We knew the work was about a fundamental shift in how people thought, ultimately letting go of control and embracing learning as living or learning as leading—the best leaders are the best learners. That's a radical shift in mind-set. It's easy to say, but it contradicts most images of leaders as people in control, people at the top of the pyramid who project this image of being forceful and dramatic and, "I've got the answer. Otherwise nobody will follow me." As opposed to the person in position of authority helping organize things and build a culture so we can actually accomplish [what we want] and learn as we go, so we can accomplish more.

We knew from the beginning that this represented a radical shift in mind-set. So we went back to a very old idea—*metanoia*. *Noia*, as from the Greek *nous* and *meta*, as in moving beyond. It means a fundamental movement or shift in mind. We started using the term because it was very clear from our initial experiences working with people [who were making this shift] that they had a profoundly different point of view. They were much more oriented toward their connections with each other and the larger world. They were much more open. They knew they weren't in control. They were trying to do as good a job as they could, but they knew they were not in control in any total sense, and they were really on a journey of becoming human beings.

The word *metanoia* was what was eventually translated in the Catholic corpus as "repent," but it was apparently the word that was actually used in expressions like, *"Metanoia, metanoia*—the kingdom of God is at hand." You must have a shift of mind or you'll never see it. It is a key in the Christian tradition. Today, at a global level, we've got to separate this from any particular religious tradition. We're at a point where we can see that nothing will really change unless there is a very fundamental movement of mind.

It's not easy. I think what's going to spur this are the breakdowns we see all around us. If we look, we can see that our mainstream ways of operating are simply not going to work much longer. We're destabilizing the climate. We're destroying ecosystems around the world. Youth unemployment is arguably the single biggest social issue in the world, which lies beneath all the social turmoil—like the terrorism. It's not the organizers of the terrorism who are the problem. It's the recruits, young people with no future because they grow up in societies that have no real ability to create meaningful paths for them. Whether you look at it from a social perspective, or from an ecological or biological perspective, or just look at our state of happiness, we are on a path to nowhere. Yet outside the mainstream, all these amazing things are happening. So this basic shift becomes more and more necessary and today, it becomes more and more possible.

Edward D. Hess

Dr. Edward Hess is professor of business administration and Batten executive-in-residence at the Darden Graduate School of Business. The author of 11 books, including *Learn or Die: Using Science to Build a Leading-Edge Learning Organization*, Dr. Hess received the Wachovia Award for Research Excellence. He currently focuses his research on innovation systems and organizational learning cultures, behaviors, and processes.

What is the difference between learning and training?

Training is a type of learning. The first part is learning *how* to do something. The second part is, "Okay, I'm learning how to do something. But to do it well takes practice, practice, practice."

Great athletes—why do they practice every day? That practice is training. They're working on specific skills. My friend Anders Ericsson at Florida State University found that it takes 10,000 hours of real deliberate, intentional practice to learn a new skill. Real focus, not, "Okay I'm doing this over and over again." It's not like when I'm scrambling an egg. It's "am I moving the fork this way so I can get the right swirl?" So training involves learning, and it also involves practice. You can learn by reading, you can learn by writing, you can learn through conversation. You can learn by experimentation, and you can learn by training.

How did you become a better and faster learner?

I became a very good, fast learner when I was very young, although it wasn't until I got much, much older that I would say I became a really good learner. I was raised in an environment where I felt that I was loved and respected if I was smart. But I grew up in a small, rural town in South Georgia where football was king. I was sort of a nerdy fat little kid. In the second grade I was the only kid in my town that did not make Pop Warner football. You don't know what that means in a small Georgia town. I was devastated. But I figured out, "Wait a minute, I'm going to learn in the classroom," and so I trained myself to be the kid that everyone hated. I was the kid in the front row. When the teacher raised a question, I would raise my hand and push my hand back and forth before she was even finished, and she had to call on me because my hand was going faster and faster. And I had the answer.

Beginning in the third grade, I developed this ability to concentrate, memorize, and think quickly. I became a thinking "machine." And that took me all the way to Wall Street. Was I a good critical thinker? No. Was I really innovative? No. Was I a good listener? No. Did I have good emotional intelligence? No. But I was a little bit like in the old Western days, the fastest gun in the saloon. And most of the time I had the right answers.

The transition to being what I would call a good learner came through adversity and failures. In the sense of developing emotional intelligence: "I need to quit interrupting people. I need to really listen. I need to be open-minded. I need to learn how to think critically and test what I believe against data and reality." I needed to learn how to de-couple my sense of self-worth, to quiet my ego. I had to learn how to be very mindful or present in a nonjudgmental manner. I'm still on that journey. I'm still a work in process.

That's interesting because so many people think that if they're going to be successful in the business world, they need to pump up their ego and they really need to project a lot of ego.

You need to believe, "I can." That doesn't need to get to the point of arrogance or puffed ego. I've reached the stage where I believe that humility is the most basic fundamental attribute necessary to be a great learner and a lifelong learner.

What is the central theme of _Learn or Die_?

That your ability to learn and the quality of your learning as an individual or an organization will basically be the primary factor in your ability to stay relevant and competitive.

The book has two purposes. One, how can you or I as individuals be a better learner? Two, what type of work environment enables and promotes human learning the best? As a result, how do I create a learning organization? An organization that continuously creates value for stakeholders, especially for customers, better and faster in a highly changing world than the competition.

Will reading the book make you a better learner? No, because it takes more work than just reading a book. Will reading the book give you things to work on, to practice, a checklist to use that lets you grade yourself daily so you can be on the journey? Yes.

I thought that Erick Brynjolfsson, the coauthor of *The Second Machine Age*, which was a great book, said it well. He said that *Learn or Die*, in effect, presents a blueprint for how to build the organization of the future, a creative, innovative organization.

In the book, you talk about the importance of having the right people, the right environment, and the right processes. So how do you put this in place?

I take a very behavioral approach to learning. Let's assume for a moment that great learners are people who are open-minded, good listeners; know how to think critically and be innovative. Thinking critically means we're willing to test our beliefs and have other people challenge us. We're open to looking for facts which disagree. We're not going to be defensive. We seek out feedback and debate. We are, if you will, always trying to improve.

So let's start with those behaviors, the ones we want to teach and train. What kind of culture do we need? The research shows that the culture needs to be a positive, emotional environment. You need high employee emotional engagement, which means the environment must meet the basic human needs of autonomy, relatedness, and effectiveness. The culture must be one of candor, with permission to speak freely. Hierarchy is devalued. Hierarchy gets in the way of learning, debate, critical thinking, [and] innovation.

I have also got to take a different view of mistakes. Mistakes are learning opportunities because the two biggest inhibitors of learning are ego and fear. So my culture's got to mitigate ego, and it's got to mitigate fear, fear of trying and fear of making mistakes (so long as mistakes are within financial parameters). Mistakes are learning opportunities. . . . If I'm making the same mistake over and over again, I should be held accountable. [Learning] organizations have mutual accountability, not just accountability up. . . . If you are my manager, you have the obligation and right to hold me accountable for my behavior . . . but I also have the obligation to hold you accountable. That's a change in corporate America.

Michael Marquardt

Dr. Michael Marquardt, president of the World Institute for Action Learning, is professor of human resource development and international affairs and program director of Overseas Programs at George Washington University. An international speaker and consultant, he has held senior management, training, and marketing positions with such organizations as Grolier, the American Society for Training and Development (ASTD, now the Association of Talent Development, or ATD), Association Management Inc., Overseas Education Fund, TradeTec, and the U.S. Office of Personnel Management. Dr. Marquardt has trained more than 95,000 managers in nearly 100 countries since beginning his international experience in Spain in 1969. His 22 books include *Organizational Learning*, *Action Learning in Action*, *The Global Learning Organization*, and *Building the Learning Organization*.

In your book, you talk about a systems learning organizational model. Tell us a little about that and what it entails.
When I began my research, I looked at what organizations around the world did best, and I discovered there were five generic areas

in which great organizations did things very well, where they learned and continuously improved. So I developed a systems model that recognized the complexity of the workplace and competitors and so forth. There are five different systems that have to be integrated simultaneously for learning organizations to be fully effective and fully powerful.

The first [system] is the learning itself. A learning organization makes learning the center of its existence. There are all types of learning: learning we gain from experience; learning we gain from planning; anticipatory learning; and learning we gain from being reflective and conscious of what's happening while it's happening. We all call it action learning. So you learn while you're in action. All those elements are key. You have to learn at the individual, group and organizational levels. I think the key learning skill is the ability to do systems thinking, systems learning. So you can identify the essence of a problem and identify the strategies that work. We have to be able to learn through dialogue and questions.

The second system is how the organization itself is structured and its vision, its values. An organization that's committed to continuous learning has strategies that encourage learning. If you want people in your organization to commit to learning, you have to reward their learning. A learning organization recognizes that actions or results are only short term, whereas learning can be applied continuously. So when people have their performance appraisal, you not only ask them what results they've produced but what they've learned that enables them to be more productive; what they've learned that they've contributed to the other members of the organization. You have to reward people for taking time to share their knowledge or learning with the other people in the organization.

If knowledge is your most important asset, you have to enable the knowledge and avoid structures or polices or hierarchy that slows or filters it . . . is to be avoided. Learning organizations have to change so that they have learning places as opposed to workplaces. You see people around you as fellow learners, as opposed to fellow workers. So that's the second system, the organization itself.

Third is people. Everyone from the leader to every employee, the vendors, suppliers in the community, have to be involved. Because what good is it if you have great leaders and great employees but your supplier is a nonlearning organization—slow, ineffective, poor quality. If your dealers are not able to sell the great product that you developed at a good cost and so forth.

Fourth is the knowledge itself. Learning organizations have to find the best ways to acquire knowledge from other sources—best practices, conferences, research. They have to create new knowledge. They have to have environments and reward systems that encourage creativity and give people an opportunity to create new knowledge. You have to store knowledge so that people throughout the organization can find it, when they need it. You have to continuously assess that knowledge so that you either retain it, get rid of it, or convert it into a higher form of knowledge such as wisdom and expertise.

The final system is the technology. Technology has two major purposes. One is to increase the spirit and quality of learning of every employee and every leader in your organization, whether it's through mobile learning, Internet learning, whatever way to get the learning to be exciting, relevant, and valuable. Technology also has to manage all that knowledge that is gained and needs to be reacquired and so forth.

That's briefly the learning organization model that I've developed over the years.

How does action learning actually build learning organizations?
Let me first describe what action learning is. It's a group of people who have been testing an urgent or complex problem. While they

are working on this problem, they are not only developing strategies and actions, they are developing their leadership skills, their team skills, and their organizational skills. Solving the problems is beneficial. But developing these lifelong learning skills and leadership skills while they're working on this individual problem can [benefit your whole] organization.

Becoming a learning organization, everyone in your organization is continuously learning. So they get a challenge and say: "What do I have to learn in order to do it better than I've done it in the past or to do it for the first time?" Action learning does it in a group because you realize complex problems cannot be solved by the leader or the individual. They can only be solved by a group.

These people change their values, they change their assumptions, they have skills that they apply on a day-to-day basis. As they work in an action learning group, they see what structures are important from an organizational perspective. They see strategies that will help them learn. They engage the community, the suppliers, or other resources. In action learning you capture ideas, strategies, knowledge that you can apply not only to the problem you're working on but the other parts of your organization. You can begin practicing action learning within 15 minutes, and the application of it can be for the rest of the life of the individuals in the group or in your organization.

What can leaders do to encourage people to engage in these behaviors, to give them responsibility? You talk a lot about the importance of giving them freedom in a room. Can you tell us more?

A leader has to always look for and create opportunities for learning. For example, [suppose] you came into my office with a problem or a question and said: "What should I do?" If I'm concerned about getting results, I would say: "Well, here is what you should do." But if I am concerned about learning, I would ask you questions and I'd say: "What are some of your ideas? Why do you think that would work?" I've [helped you] develop your skills and capabilities, and confidence.

When I have a meeting as a leader, instead of spending all the time with results and policies and sharing information, we take time to learn. I say: "Has anyone here created success this past week? How were you able to do that? Does anyone have a challenge that the rest of us could work at [so we can] develop skills as a team?" I think leaders have to see themselves as coaches, mentors, and teachers. That's the most important role in a learning organization.

You say there are eight significant forces that necessitate a shift to learning organization models. Can you talk about those significant forces?

The first force, obviously, is globalization and global competition. You have to learn because you now are competing with the best organizations from around the world. I think the second major change has been the impact of technology. Twenty years ago the Internet was just beginning. We did not have smartphones or mobile learning. Technology has dramatically changed the environment. The third is that the work world has changed dramatically. People don't go to the office to work. Or they work for a number of different organizations at the same time. They may have several bosses or no bosses. They may be working more closely with a supervisor.

A fourth difference is that customers have much more power because of technology and global competition and so forth. We used to go to the local store to buy a book. Now I can order a book, or any service I want, online. I have much more power as a customer so I want the best price. I want to customize to my needs. I want innovative things that can prepare me for the future. I want high quality and, if anything goes wrong, I want it to be fixed immediately at a low cost. This is putting lot of pressure on organizations to learn.

I think a fifth [force] is that what we do in organizations is really different. We used that term called "manufacture," that monstrous work with hands and machines. But now most of the work that we do is with our brains, we call it "mentalfacturing." The monstrous are knowledge workers, and we spend much of our day in learning to prepare for an interview or a customer, to handle a project. Most of our day now is spent in learning for some particular event or action.

Another challenge or force is that the workers, particularly the best, have high expectations. They have the ability to work on their own or work for other organizations via the technology. To retain and attract these top workers, the organization has to have an environment which gives them the opportunity to learn, to be creative, to have impact.

A seventh is that there's more diversity in the workplace. We have people from all different cultures, short-term, long-term, all types of experiences, and they have to work together.

The final force is that we have complexity in the world. We cannot understand it by linear thinking. We have to do what we call systems thinking [so we can] understand that complexity, understand that things change very rapidly and everything that is done impacts other things. I think these eight forces have resulted in organizations needing to continuously learn and improve. Or else they'll die.

Hank Paulson Jr.

Henry Paulson Jr. was the seventy-fourth secretary of the treasury under President George W. Bush, from July 2006 to January 2009. Before that, he had a 32-year career at Goldman Sachs, serving as chairman and chief executive officer.

What made you successful?

There are a number of things that are important to success. Intellectual curiosity is important. There are a lot of smart people who are motivated and want to do well. But people who are self-aware and understand their strengths and their weaknesses and work to improve themselves, and who put people around them who help them play to their strengths and compensate for their weaknesses, make a big difference. Learning is a huge part of success. I say that to every young professional as they are beginning their first job. More important than anything is learning.

What is your definition of *learning*?

I tend to be someone who learns by doing. For instance, I learn through writing. I don't care how well you think you know something, when you've got to put it down on paper, to explain it to others, that takes it to a different level. I learn by watching others. I learn through making mistakes. But I also enjoy some very simple forms of learning. I go birding with my wife and I take a bird book and I can say, "That is a Paradise Tanager up there and the reason you know that it is a female and not a male is by looking at that little marking on the side or by listening to the song." Or when I go saltwater fly fishing I learn from a guide who tells me how to do it.

Gary Beach

Gary Beach has been in the technology media business since 1981. He served in management roles at McGraw-Hill, where he worked on the world's first data networking magazine, *Data Communications*, and he was publisher of the International Data Group's *Network World*, *Computerworld*, and *CIO* magazines. For the past 10 years, he has written a column on tech talent in the print edition of *CIO* magazine and has done technology commentary for National Public Radio's *All Things Considered* and *Morning Edition*. In 1994, Beach founded Tech Corps, a national nonprofit dedicated to challenging information technology (IT) executives to get involved in K–12 education in America. He has also been a member of the board of directors for Net Day. He is the author of *The U.S. Technology Skills Gap*.

What do you see as the relevance of third-party training organizations to help assess an organization in terms of skills and then helping to improve those skills?

I think they're critical. Accenture recently did a study that said in the last five years, 80 percent of companies offered no corporate training and development. None! Zero! That's unconscionable, and it's got to change. If they don't have the time because staff is lean and they're out visiting customers, they need to leverage partnerships with third-party training organizations. The key, I think, is that the CIO has to identify what he or she thinks the skills they'll need twenty-four, thirty-six months out, and then go out and partner with groups to teach and train their employees.

Why did you write *The U.S Technology Skills Gap*? If you were going to write a tweet about the central theme of the book, what would it say?

I often get asked that question. It's because CIOs were starting to share their thoughts about the difficulty of hiring men and women with the skills they needed. I was at a conference in Cincinnati. A speaker read this quote: "Our nation is at risk. We're swimming in a sea of mediocrity. If another country did what we're doing to our education system, we would consider it an act of war."

To borrow from Confucius, the central theme of the book is "If a country wants one year of prosperity, grow grain. If you want ten years of prosperity, grow a tree. If you want one hundred years of prosperity, grow people." The book is all about the importance of growing people, particularly in the busy, globally connected environment that we're all working in right now.

Bertrand Moingeon

Professor of strategic management, Bertrand Moingeon is the author and editor of numerous books and publications, including *Organizational Learning and Competitive Advantage*, one of the first books on this topic. Since 2007 he has been the deputy dean of HEC Paris, a business school, in charge of executive education and academic development. He is also the cofounder and director of the HEC Europe Institute and has been a visiting research scholar at Harvard Business School. Professor Moingeon was awarded the honorable distinctions of *Chevalier dans l'Ordre du Mérite* and *Chevalier dans l'Ordre des Palmes Académiques* for his academic and managerial achievements.

What is the central theme or thesis of your excellent book, *Organizational Learning and Competitive Advantage*?
Our main ambition was to bridge organizational behavior and strategy. The simple idea is that competitive advantage can be obtained by focusing on the human factor and *learning capabilities*. In fact it's faster to develop a low-cost strategy or to introduce the innovations that will provide you competitive advantage, but it is not sustainable. The real source of competitive advantage is to introduce innovation or the capacity to be cost-effective in the long term, in an ongoing way.

Years ago I had a conversation with CEO of a company that was making handset mobile telephones. He was very proud of his new mobiles. He said, "This is the killer mobile with which we're going to have a huge success." In fact, they had huge success for six months; the year after, the product disappeared. That's the indication that one innovation is very often not enough. What is required is the capacity to innovate, what we call Learning Capability. In this case he didn't have this learning capability. I think it is [even] more relevant today.

How do you define *learning organization* today?

The broad term is "*organizational learning*," and there are different ways to study it. For instance, people have studied what we call *organizational routines* and how those routines become part of the memory of the organization. So learning is basically to create new routines that would be part of the memory of the organization. If we think about an airline company, people may leave but the way to operate and how to fly an airplane it is based on routines that are independent of people. That's one field of research. The other field of research is how to build what we call learning organizations. The ambition is to produce actionable knowledge that can be used by the leaders to make change happen in their organizations.

I want to be more precise about the word *learning*. Technically, learning occurs when members of an organization identify a problem. They identify the gap and they correct it. No learning organization would make the same errors again and again. Unfortunately, it's quite common to see organizations that don't learn. They repeat the same problems, the same errors.

I mentioned that it's identifying the gap between what I did and what I wanted to do but it's also looking into the future, identifying the gap between what I would like to do [and what I'm doing now]. That can be, "What kind of company would I like to build? Where are we today?" This is also a part of the way we define "*learning organization*."

What do you mean by "learning how" and "learning why"?

Learning How refers to the capability to improve processes in companies. Nowadays [we have] the Internet of Things or the

Internet of Everything, combined with Big Data. We have new hot topics that can be used to develop a new kind of operational effectiveness or operational excellence. Learning How refers to doing more of the same but doing it better. It's what we call the *logic of exploitation*: We know how to do things but we're going to exploit it and we're going to do it better.

Learning Why is the capability to diagnose complex situations, test new ideas, experiment, and innovate. Learning Why refers not to the logic of exploitation but to the logic of *exploration*. The capacity to explore new territories, new opportunities. Learning Why is required when you want to design disruptive innovations, for instance.

Nowadays the environment [is] so unpredictable, so complex, that the Learning Why capability is more critical than what it was before. The old recipes don't work anymore. [Learning Why] is not doing more of the same; it's the capacity to revisit the way you manage the company.

What type of learning methods do you think should be used generally in an organization? Or is it different for everyone?
I would advocate that companies use a mix of formal and informal learning. What I mean by formal learning is to set up sessions, working with business schools to develop executive programs in order to promote learning. Informal learning is to encourage people to share what they learn, to actively contribute to knowledge management and learning within the company.

From the perspective of the business schools, I think we need to move from the model of being professors, being the wise people on stage, to acting as guides. We should promote learning by leveraging what people already know. When you facilitate a program [with 30 people], very often you have 600 years of accumulated experience in the room. The role of the professor is to leverage those 600 years of experience to the benefit of collective learning. If you just preach, people will not necessarily learn. People will learn through the interaction between the research that the professor's done and sharing what they already know and what they've already experienced. A knowledge-sharing forum is very key to promote learning.

Why do you think the lifelong learning journey is so important?
Because learning is life. We need to equip people not with techniques that will be obsolete in a couple of months or a few years or a few days but with learning capabilities and the willingness to learn during all their lives.

Learning Managers and Learning Professionals

Roseanna DeMaria

Roseanna DeMaria, the chief learning officer at the NYU School of Professional Studies, is the founder and principal of DeMaria Group, a consulting firm dedicated to optimizing company, team, and individual performance. Her more than 20 years of business and management experience ranges from government to start-ups to Fortune 500 corporations, including Merrill Lynch and AT&T. She has consistently achieved industry and board recognition for her leadership skills and business results, and her strategy, innovation, and values-based approach to people development has been studied, admired, and imitated. She serves on the advisory boards of forward-thinking, innovative start-ups that think differently and deliver unique value in business and education.

How do you measure the ROI of learning?
One problem is that we've taken to measuring training by the number of programs we offered, how many people have taken them, and what they cost. Figuring out an ROI in a very

transactional rubric. What you really want to measure is whether people are going out and doing what you've trained them to do. In a customer service model, whether your calls are getting answered faster. Like Welch said, that's what you want to measure.

The pushback on my position could be, "Hey Roseanna, how do you measure whether a leader has gotten better?" Well, you can look at their 360s, you can look at whether their people are producing more, but at the end of the day there is no meter that will say this leader now has this much EQ versus that much EQ. It's about the perceptions of the people around them of their performance. The minute you start getting away from true performance results related to the business, you're probably getting more and more unable to have a good look at the impact.

Why is it important for businesses to be learning organizations?
It's not important if the business doesn't have to change, if the business does one thing, and there's always a market for that one thing. But we know that there is no business like that anymore. So if you are not learning, you can't be competitive. You can't even see what's coming toward you. What good is it to build the best buggy whip for a horse and buggy when cars are the disruptive innovation on the landscape? If you truly are committed to taking your organization to the next level, you have to make sure you're not building the best buggy whip.

A learning organization allows people to thrive and allows the business to thrive because it will never settle. I like to use the term *"restless excellence,"* because restlessness is saying, "What are we doing well today and how can we be better?" That's different than *"ongoing improvement."* It means being willing to blow up the model and think about things differently. That's what learning organizations do, because they're willing to question themselves, to question their assumptions. That's hard to do when you're being successful.

In your article, "Performance DNA," you talk about a "focus fire fate fear." Can you share that framework with us?

I think the F word is critical in performance and right talent and the F word that I'm talking about is *focus*—being able to focus on problems proactively. Stay focused on a goal with the flexibility to know that it may change. Can you stay focused when you are under attack, when the goal is a hard-stretch goal to reach? I think focus is critical. *Fire* is the passion—that engine that never goes out. You can be in a rainstorm and high-performance fire never gets wet.

This is not fear in a paralyzing way. It's really fear of disappointing yourself or others. I know it's not caché to say leaders need to be feared. Well-feared command and control leaders—some are successful, some are not. I don't think that leadership style is healthy because it inhibits creativity. But if a leader is respected, there has to be an underlying fear: The performer doesn't want to disappoint the leader because they care about the leader. Typically, the hotter the fire, the higher the fear because you are driven to succeed.

Did you have a framework you used in Merrill Lynch to double up individualized learning plans for your team and for the organization?

We always started with the business need. One need was that we had managers who never had any formal training in management. So we built a program around them that was relevant to the business.

In terms of individual development, we launched a performance management system that tied back to Merrill Lynch University. When a manager sat down with an employee to discuss the development plan for the year, they could electronically access an electronic menu of available courses. They would identify the employee's need and then see what currently existed.

Online is very powerful because it can be anywhere, and you can update it in real time. We created a new employee orientation so that if you were having your first day in Tokyo, you would have the same online orientation as someone starting in Akron, Ohio. I think those tools are really useful; they solve a business need.

What do you think made you successful?

I think that to be successful, you have to take the long, hard journey to figure out where you are in this life, who you are, and what your values are. That journey never ends. But if you can go deep inside yourself and decide who you are, who you want to be, and then be very passionate about living it, it all comes together. You have to have the competence, you have to be committed, and then you have to have the infrastructure to support it. Many times people will say, what is your biggest personal success? What's your biggest business success? What's your biggest personal failure, your biggest business failure? That suggests there are two segments of me—that I am someone else in my personal life than I am in my business life. When I die, Russell, there's going to be one gravestone, not two, and if I'm true and I accomplish what I want in this life, it's going to say that she made a difference to the people in the businesses she touched. Sometimes we think we can be two different people. When you do that, you go down a very slippery slope that leads to disaster.

Alison Cunard

Alison Cunard is the general manager of Microsoft Learning Experiences, a training and skills development organization that helps individuals and organizations worldwide maximize the use of Microsoft technologies to realize their full potential. Before joining Microsoft, she was a principal consultant at Oracle and a software engineer at Ford Aerospace.

What does the phrase "learning is transformation" mean to you?

I've been around the world on behalf of Microsoft, talking about the importance of learning. What we've seen is that when we provide great learning assets and great learning opportunities in cultures where people are really, really interested in learning, it transforms their lives. Learning can be that transformation element that really propels people into a future of success and prosperity. It's super heartwarming to see how that can happen.

If you're not learning and growing, how can you possibly innovate? And how can you take advantage of other people's innovations? What we see is people learning from others' failures and others' successes, and being able to innovate on top of others' innovations.

Personally, I'm learning how to ride a mountain bike, which seems easy but it's not. It's very technical and requires learning to use lots of equipment. On the professional side, I decided to get certified on a Microsoft technology myself, so I could go through the process our customers go through. I read the book, I signed up for the practice exam and took it several times, and I went through the whole process of what happens after you're certified. That was great learning for me, not only from a perspective of learning a skill, but learning what our customers experience from our products.

What made you successful? How did you get to be the general manager of Microsoft Learning Experiences?

One thing that has really helped me succeed is passion. I've always made it a goal to love what I do, to be passionate about what I do every day. With that passion comes energy, and with that energy you can continue to learn and grow. That passion enables you to do the next thing in your career, because you're passionate about that next thing.

Why did you choose a career in the learning industry?

I enjoy the field of learning because I can see firsthand how we can change lives. This role is very much about making a difference in how people can succeed. We can change their economic prosperity, and even the prosperity of a nation, through the assets we're developing and through partners like you. That makes me feel very good. It's satisfying from a job perspective, and it's challenging. Technology is driving many, many changes in the learning industry, so the challenges are there and the satisfaction is there.

Why do you think there is a skills gap, especially in the United States? How can organizations solve that problem?

The skills gap is a complex, frustrating problem. Microsoft alone has thousands and thousands of open jobs for IT professionals, and many companies do. On the other side we see an unemployment problem in certain sectors in the United States.

What a company can do is continue to invest in their people. One of the reasons we are in this situation is that companies aren't investing in their talent, to grow that talent within the organization and keep their skills up to date. If they'd been making those investments, we would have fewer people who are unemployed and unable to get those new jobs in the technology space.

The other thing is that not enough people are going into technology fields in college in this country. That's not news. There's work we need to do as a nation around driving technology interest at younger levels in elementary schools, in middle schools. High school is too late. It's got to be done younger, when technology is fun and interesting to girls and to boys, so we can drive interest in those careers before they decide they don't want to do them once they're in high school. That would help our skills gap tremendously, but we have to start young. It's too late once they're in college to convert them to an IT field.

Tom Evans

Former CLO of PricewaterhouseCoopers (PwC), Tom Evans was the driving force behind the everyday development of PwC's U.S. staff, dedicated to cultivating and advancing the firm's culture of ongoing professional development. Tom is a pioneering leader in breaking down the walls of traditional classroom education and integrating learning into the workplace. He helped create an immersive and inclusive development journey that keeps PwC's people challenged, motivated, and inspired to invest in their own development and that of others, and he positioned the learning and development team as a trusted partner and integral driver in executing PwC's business and human capital strategies. In October 2014, Tom received *Chief Learning Officer*'s prestigious CLO of the Year award. He is a former advisory board member for Duke University's Center for Leadership and Ethics and a member of the Association of the U.S. Army, the American Society for Training & Development now called the Association for Talent Development, or ATD) and the American Institute of Certified Public Accountants. He retired from PwC in 2015.

How do you build a culture that helps build learning within the organization?

It starts for us on Day One. The first day, you are engaged. It is also important that there is an aspect that is behavioral. You can share with someone what you value; you can share what you feel is proper behavior; you can discuss accountability; you can discuss what your capability sets are; but at some point it is important to understand how you can experience those. That's what we do starting on Day One, and from that day it is reinforced whenever our people come together.

It's not just within the development organization, but it is a broader part of the core of [our] human capital strategy—being accountable and a keeper of culture, recognizing how you employ technology, how you look at your talent pools, and the influence of turnover on your talent pools, you can always have those influences. So it is a broader human capital strategy, but within the function of learning, it is present as everything that we do.

Tell us a little about how globalization and technology have changed the way things work in a learning organization.

Technology is always going to be a challenge. It is easy to simply say, "Go after the technology," because it's there. [But] understanding the human need to be social, there is a balance that needs to be maintained. So the opportunity for technology, used in a smart way, can do wonders for advancing your opportunity to accelerate someone's development and do that at a reasonable, affordable cost. Naturally, in a globalized environment, having the ability and the opportunity to do that and capitalize on the value of that is going to continue to expand.

How does PwC manage the learning operation in terms of content, delivery, technology, and administration?

Given our scale, we do have an LMS and we do use social media sites. We have an internal site we call Spark, and we also have a call center. Wherever you are, whatever your business is, you can contact that call center and get information that you need, especially around the execution of things. So if you're enrolling in a program or something else, you have the convenience of that access.

Structurally, we are centralized within one function, whether it is a particular business need or whether it is core and central to the firm [such as] technical ability, leadership ability, relationships, acumen. This includes things that are regulatory and compliance based. How you employ those in an efficient way falls under one central PwC organization.

Do you find that there are any skill-gap issues when you are hiring for PwC?

I think you always find them. In Data Analytics, it is important to understand how data is going to leverage itself in the future and what that means, and how organizations can capitalize on that. Everybody is looking at that.

But when you have individuals who are very capable with technology, how do you help challenge their ability to problem solve? How do you help them avoid the risks associated with multitasking versus task switching? The executive function of the brain can only do one thing well at a time. Helping someone build their acumen and understanding in today's environment, what does that mean? Whether it is your social acumen or your business acumen or your global acumen, how do you define that? The complexity of engagement today is increasing, so I see that as another area which will continue to evolve. The technical areas are always there, and you are always going to have basic fixing when you need it. But these broader areas are the most interesting to me, and I think they are the ones we will face in the future.

How much of your instruction is now classroom versus online or remote?

We generally don't give it a percentage, but by the nature of what we do, we have more face-to-face learning than technology. It is important for us to understand that from the standpoint of the culture, the business-development opportunities, and the social elements of our firm.

How we're using the space and how we're blending within that space has evolved quite a bit. So while face-to-face is still a significant portion of what we do, how we're doing it is changing. As someone said, when we blend, we aren't making a smoothie. It is important that we understand the nature of the new blend so that we can blend technology into it. This is a significant factor leading to success.

At a very simple level, I think that how technology is evolving gives you an opportunity to step back and look at how you are using that physical space today. Can you make it more simulation based? Can you make it more behavioral? Can you use technology to flip it? This is important, because the nature of technology says that I can do things using a different media that gets my folks more prepared and engaged.

This also puts a higher premium on the use of physical space to accomplish more. Technology provides an amazing opportunity to think through what that means for any organization and how they do it. It's a way to bring people together, but the ROI associated with what you have accomplished has improved dramatically. So thinking about blending and technology leads to the question of how can you use those things to create the most significant benefit to the individual and to the organization? That's the deeper aspect, the more behavioral aspect of learning.

Tell us how you measure success of your learning and development programs.

Today more than ever, understanding how you measure impact is increasingly important. It is valuable from a training standpoint; it is most valuable if you want to be seen as a leader who is sitting at the executive table, trying to solve the same problem [with] the human capital of the organization that the CEO is trying to solve. If you want to be relevant, you have to embrace it.

The Kirkpatrick scale is there and we use it. Our measurement is geared around some very simple things: "Like it, learn it, live it, leverage it" is the quote we play with. The importance is that there is a certain value proposition, because if they like it, they will learn it. The question is, are they applying it? That is where the difference occurs. So not only do we employ the natural measurements from standards, but we investigate thoroughly what the application is on the job and how that contributes to things that are measurable and important to our business.

[For example,] how do you measure effective turnover? Do you look at leverage? How do you look at connectivity? How do you understand whether or not people see what they are doing as being meaningful? Are they passing it on and actually employing it in work with others? Therefore, we do more immersive studies, and we do them over time—not only at the point of completion, or at the beginning and end of the program, but in a way that is naturally elongated for those areas that we measure.

Dave DeFilippo

Dave DeFilippo is currently the CLO for Suffolk Construction. Previously, he was CLO for the Bank of New York (BNY) Mellon and a member of the company's operating committee and diversity and inclusion council. He led BNY Mellon's L&D strategy as part of the company's BNY Mellon University, which is aimed at fostering an active learning culture across the firm and its more than 50,000 employees worldwide. DeFilippo, who has been recognized with several industry awards, regularly speaks and writes about topics related to leadership development, executive coaching, and learning and talent management.

How do you define a learning organization?
A learning organization is one that is focused on achieving its maximum performance, aspiring to reach its potential, and ultimately, through trial and error, learning how to self-correct so it doesn't repeat the same mistakes.

How do you build and maintain a learning culture within an organization?

The best way is to start off being very, very clear about the business requirements, then to build a structure, a team, and processes that support them. One of the places that I see the best laid plans fail is not having appropriate leadership support and a sustainability strategy.

What behaviors do you promote within the organization to help build a learning culture? How do you define the right leaders and the right people?

The first thing I look for is passion. That the people on the team really care about the organization, about helping our employees learn and optimize their performance and potential.

After passion, I look for someone who comes to work every day and wants to make a difference. Someone who wants to change things. Instead of thinking about the current state being satisfactory, they think about a better future state.

The last thing that's really important is that we collaborate and we work together. The best ideas, the best learning as a team, happens through that collaborative process.

Do you think that there's a skills gap in the IT industry?

What we see in the workforce is that it's definitely more challenging to fill highly specific information technology roles. We definitely see that as a macro challenge. We're addressing that challenge by focusing on the job-specific skills that are needed and doing an assessment process so that we know what the current state is and what future state we desire, and on hiring and developing people to fill those gaps. It's a work in progress, but we believe it's the right thing to do, especially for this segment that's so important.

If this experiment works well, we could scale that process across other job families, right? If that works in IT, why not do that with our client-facing people? Why not do that across leaders and managers to ensure we have the right people leading and managing our staff?

You've said your experience as a track coach and a teacher has helped you appreciate the link between learning and performance. Tell us more about that.

Back when I was a teacher and a coach, it was important to help everyone on that team have a goal and try every year or every season to improve on that goal. If you think about that in the context of an organization, we have different positions, we have different teams. If we can get the collective performance of the organization to increase from where it is today to where we want it to be in the future, it's like someone jumping 13 feet in the long jump and the next year they want to jump 14 feet. Doing that year after year and season after season—that's when I've seen organizations and teams reach their potential.

What advice would you give to someone who's looking to become a learning leader?

First start in a business role, and if you don't start in a business role, at least rotate into a business role at some point. I think the perspective of what it's like to be a front-line employee or a first-line manager will pay dividends throughout one's whole career; I know it has for me.

The other thing is that I would encourage people to get grounded in some of the key foundations of learning—learning theory, adult learning styles, instructional design, learning technology. Learn all those things, have a point of view about them, and incorporate that point of view into your beliefs about learning.

Karen Kocher

As the CLO for Cigna, Karen Kocher is accountable for learning, leadership effectiveness, and organizational development for the entire Cigna team as well as for external stakeholders. She oversees capability and competency development, strategic workforce planning, employee engagement, and the redesign of Cigna's performance management model.

Before joining Cigna, Karen worked at IBM in multiple roles, including as Global Solutions executive in the Software division and offering executive for advanced and emerging technologies in Global Services, and she has been the general manager/vice president and P&L leader for the IKON Office Solution's New England Learning Services business. She earned the prestigious Chartered Property Casualty Underwriter (CPCU) designation from the American College and is a member of the CPCU Society.

What would you say is your biggest challenge as chief learning officer in an organization that employs 35,000 people globally? What do you do to meet that challenge?

Most days the biggest challenge is staying one step ahead of the business. My job is to make sure we have talent that's capable of doing all that we want or need to do in advance of the business. If we don't have the skill and knowledge to do something that needs to be done today, then we are going to be behind. And we can't afford to be behind.

I do it by being a continuous learner. I read an incredible array of magazines and websites and white papers, and I talk to an unknown number of people. I see it as my job to observe as much content as I possibly can, delineate what's really important, and then act on what's important and bring it to other people's attention. That's how I think I'm successful in this role.

What is your overall learning mission?

Our whole learning mission is to make sure we have the right capabilities in the organization to deliver on the business strategy. Parallel with that, we provide the necessary resources and support and tools for individuals to realize their current ambitions. We figure that if we can be successful with both of those, we will be successful as an organization. For the most part, we are doing very well on the ability to align with business strategies and help the company be successful. I think we have more work that we need to do to help people appreciate and deliver on their current ambitions.

We've been focused on several activities over the past year. First, to identify the employee engagement result we had in 2013, that the employees felt we spent more time helping them realize their career ambitions. Then we spent about a year putting in place a lot of different resources. One that's been really successful is a career talks video series. We had a variety of individuals throughout the organization doing video talks about what they have done in their careers and how they did it. What lessons they had for others. That's been really popular.

What types of behaviors do you promote for building a learning culture?

A lot of the behaviors we promote are beneficial for a learning culture, but they are also beneficial in general. A behavior such as curiosity. Curiosity can serve somebody well in just about any facet of their life. It also happens to be necessary to be a good learner. Then you have things like optimism. If somebody is optimistic, it helps them to appreciate why other points of view may be important, which means they have a more open mind and are typically good learners. A lot of [these behaviors] don't necessarily align strictly with learning or even mostly with learning, but they are critical components of somebody having a learning mind-set and being a continuous learner.

How much does training have to be adapted to the various workforce generations?

You have to be prepared to take into consideration the personalized aspects of what people want and need. I don't know that is so much a generational thing; I think it's preferences. People prefer to learn in different ways. I think of it more as the ability to deliver options based on preferences than as a generational situation.

Tell us about your learning operation and managing content. Is content developed in-house, or do you use outside vendors?

We at Cigna University don't develop any content. We outsource all of our content development to a company we've been working with for quite a few years. The formal learning content is developed in that way.

As it relates to informal content, like career-talks videos, we do those types of things in-house. As we move more toward the less formal, we are starting to get more involved in that type of content development. We figure out what subject area is most important and go in search of the best source for content. It can range from a TED Talk to a well-based offering from, say, Columbia. We've tried to make a whole set of options available to people so they can pick and choose based on their need and the way that they prefer to learn. Most of that content is now absolutely free versus the portfolios that we used to buy from external companies that, in some cases, cost more than a million dollars.

How do you measure learning outcome? Is success tied to the bottom line, or are there other ways that you measure the outcome?

We try always to have one business-aligned measure, what we call *business-valued measure*, and then one learning-related measure. As an example, we recently did some consultative sales work outside the United States. The business-valued measure was around generating additional revenue and improving the persistency of our existing customers. So we had a couple of business-valued measures and metrics, and then we also had a couple that were related to learning effectiveness. And it's worked well. It helps us refine our learning but also helps the business appreciate whether or not they are getting value from the investment that they're making, their time, and their money.

What do you do at Cigna to make learning and development more efficient?

There are really two things. One is focus and align. Each year I work with a group of executives on an advisory board. We go through a process of deciding on the characteristics and the capabilities that are most critical for the company to be successful with its business strategy, and we prioritize them. We never commit to more than we can deal with, given our budget. This year we are focused on customer focus, change leadership, and influential leadership.

The other aspect that is really important are the approaches themselves. We've used a lot of experiential approaches. Although they are a bigger time investment for people, they tend to be less costly and more sustainable. That's helped us to be more cost-efficient.

Can you give us examples of some of your proudest moments on the job?

Some of my proudest moments are when the people on my team are able to take on different responsibilities. I get a particular delight when somebody accomplishes something they didn't think they could do. I spend a lot of my time talking to people about opportunities they can take on or projects and assignments that they can lead. At the first approach, you can note a hesitance in their voice. It's like: "Oh, Jeez. I'm not sure." You have to convince them to take it on, and then six months later you can see the look on their face when they've delivered a successful outcome. They are so incredibly pleased with themselves. It makes everything worthwhile.

Robert Burnside

Robert Burnside oversees the L&D function at Ketchum, a public relations and marketing agency that specializes in corporate and product positioning. He has extensive experience in learning and development, including corporate learning, e-learning, adult development, leadership development, and creativity and innovation, which he has applied in a variety of roles, including consulting, professional services, and executive management in the public relations industry. Before joining Ketchum, where he has been a partner since 2005, he worked with the Center for Creative Leadership (CCL), where he designed and delivered creativity and leadership programs for Global 1000 firms worldwide and brought the institution's leadership products into the online environment. He began his career as a Peace Corps volunteer (www.peacecorps.gov) in Haryana, India. Burnside's current focus is on providing just-in-time learning that provides globally relevant guidance for agency strategy on the ground. Most recently, he has overseen 1,600 client-facing employees participating in a social engagement online program called "Ketchum 2016: The Race to Make It Real," which teaches people how to build campaign-leading creative programs that deploy across all web channels, paid, earned, shared, and owned.

How do you build a culture that supports learning within an organization?

We have a basic model we call "Head, Heart, and Feet." If there's going to be any knowledge exchange between two people, there needs to be a clear concept for the head, on what you're trying to understand. Then you need two hearts—both people have to see some reason for why it's useful to learn, why it's important and interesting. For the feet, ask, "What am I going to do with this? I have a clear idea, I'd like to do it, but how do I do it?" You don't need a 1,000-page manual; you just need the first few steps.

The other components are that the people understand they can't achieve the organizational purpose without learning being central. Skill development—"how do you develop good PR?"—but also their own curiosity and growth of their ability to understand and bring a good solution to the client.

So if you want to build a learning organization, make sure the purpose of the organization is clear and the individuals see how learning is their highway to attaining their own, and the organization's, purpose.

Can you tell us how you develop a learning plan for individuals, teams, and the organization as a whole?
Let's start with the organization as a whole—that's the business strategy of the executive team. The web has dramatically changed the delivery of all marketing communications. Everybody is now a brand manager. All the various parts of marketing communication are desperately trying to be the ones who are best at conversations between the brands and their constituencies, their consumers. Public relations has a pretty big opportunity to grow, as it's always been a conversational-based communication tool.

So we are looking to help our people understand the potential growth opportunities for public relations. From a learning standpoint, the question is, "What do our people need to know to be able to see how to grow public-relation types of communication when competing against ad agencies and all the other communication agencies we compete with?" That has a learning plan.

At the individual level, we have quite a number of certificate programs. We have one called *DigiMaster*, where you can earn a certificate if you go through 18 live videos that teach 18 different aspects of communications in the digital-social sphere. If you complete all of them, we will give you a certificate that says you are a certified Digital Master, by Ketchum University. People love that. So we put those programs out there and individuals are attracted to what they think is going to best propel their career forward and best give them "*status*" with a client.

We don't try to tell an individual, "You need to do these things." They choose what is going to help them best. It always comes back to the individual. If the individual doesn't want to change, they won't, which gives me a chance to share one of my favorite quotes [paraphrased from Gandhi]: "If you want to change the world, change yourself." I really believe that. In learning and development, it really comes down to the individual choosing to grow and develop.

How much learning has to be adapted to the various cultures and generations? You have the Gen X, the Gen Y, the Millennials, and now you're operating in a global economy.

Let's start with cultural differences. From the North American standpoint, you might think that teaching your colleagues to be brash go-getters who really challenge the competition is good. That goes right against the grain for [people from] Asian cultures, who see that as very inappropriate. So your goal with those clients might not be to be brash and push back; your goal might be to help the client understand the value of our services. All our nationalities have the mind-set that "I am as I am, and why do I have to understand how these other people think?" So there's the first big one.

The generational one has been interesting, because in public relations we have quite a lot of young people. We're also about

70 percent female, 30 percent male. We have a lot of Millennials; they are more purpose-driven and more likely to leave and go to another agency if they don't see their life purpose being played out with ours. Whereas the boomer generation, my generation—we left for money or power.

Some of the differences are simply life stages: When we're in our twenties, we are learning and open and ready to move. In our thirties we are getting a little more clear on what we want to do, and by the time we hit our forties, it's time to commit. So we not only have the generational differences, but also the life stage differences and the cultural, national differences. We need to pay attention to all of those in our learning programs.

How do you measure the success of a training and development program within an organization?

We spent almost a third of our yearly budget on [our online program] The Race to Make It Real. How are we going to measure that that was a good investment? Well, we're going to see that our 2,000 people who face clients have better results, with the clients saying that our people are delivering more creative skills and are giving better access to Web communications than they were before. The client gets to say, "Yeah, I see a difference."

We also measure an internal difference: from a manager's perspective, or from the employee's perspective of "Have I learned this? Can I do this better?" and other things, such as, "Did they do the process correctly?"

But the bottom line is whether the client has seen a difference. Now, that difference can't always be related to money, especially if what you're trying to attain is, for example, a better relationship with a client. Eventually, you will expect that to result in money. But in the meantime, we want our clients to think we are easier to work with. So we would measure that, and claim it as an outcome of our learning intervention, while realizing that it's not quite bottom-line. I think a lot of learning investment is like that.

How do you pick the best learning approach for your organization?

At the individual level, a manager comes to me and says, "I need my people to know 'X.'" My first question will be to describe the problems they're trying to solve, and my next question will be "How can I help?" Before I design, I ask, "As a result of attending this learning activity that I am building, your people will be able to do *what*?" Unless they are clear on the outcome, I won't build it. But if they're clear, I will design a learning activity to get them there.

At the organizational level, it's a question of, "Where is the organization most likely to fail? What are the walls we're banging into right now?" Now the question becomes, "How can an investment in learning help to achieve a business goal, or overcome barriers, or achieve in this new area? Why is that investment better than an investment in technology, or hiring, or something else?" I design the learning function at the organizational level [as] an investment the organization makes.

T.J. Elliott

As Educational Testing Service's (ETS) vice president and CLO, T.J. Elliott has overall responsibility for those processes that share knowledge, develop people and organizations, ensure appropriate collaborative work spaces, and enable growth and innovation across the enterprise. He is charged with helping ETS implement new and better ways to work in an increasingly competitive marketplace, as well as ensuring that the organization capitalizes on the skills and talents of its employees to achieve its mission.

Coauthor of *Decision DNA: Discovering Reality Based Decision Making* (Infinity, 2005), Elliott also wrote the foreword to the second edition of *Work-Based Learning: Bridging Knowledge and Action in the Workplace* by Joseph Raelin and a chapter in 2014's *Smarter Innovation: Using Interactive Processes to Drive Better Business Results*, edited by Katrina Pugh (Ark).

How do you develop your learning plans?

Let me start with the organization. We have cascading goals, and we use a balanced scorecard approach, as Kaplan and Norton have articulated it. We know what the goals of the organization are, and we work with the chief strategy officer to understand what needs to happen from a connection and development stance.

Once we've done that, we try to separate [the goals] into what we call the *big rocks*. We have no more than seven and ideally no more than five big rocks. Then we validate them with folks from outside our unit to make sure we're not missing something from the business side by looking at these things too closely from a learning perspective. We might say, "We want a development program that actually brings people into using our learning management system more often and taking more control over their own learning." That allows us to focus our attention in a place where we're going to get the most value; otherwise, you can end up getting request after request after request, and it doesn't add up to something significant.

Individually, we use a learning management system and plan around the six ETS competencies—we call them ETS Success Six. We ask people to not only say, "Where am I in the continuum," but also to invite others to comment. We've got a setup through SharePoint where they can go in and invite two other people besides their manager to comment. That leads to a conversation: "Let me triangulate—I thought I was here, you think I'm here, you think I'm here—what do I need to focus on?"

It would be a mistake for anyone to say, "I'm going to work on getting all six of these and move across from learning to proficiency to mastery in one year." It's not going to happen. We ask people to choose, and we offer an array of ways in which they can do that.

A lot of learning is informal. Part of what we're asking people to do is consider how they can use the activities that exist within their own job to gain more learning, and that means having a more reflective attitude: How do I consider what I thought was going to happen doing that activity? Is there anything that happened differently? Do I need to change my approach the next time? A lot of learning occurs in that way, and that needs to connect to the learning plan. How does this change how I think about marketing side service orientation? How does this change how I think about relationship mastery? Is there anything I would have done differently in terms of how I worked with those folks? Do I now realize that I really need to get a hold of a negotiation course? Or I came from another industry, and I don't understand how assessments are built here, so I've got to go into all the videos. We have hundreds of hours of videos of experts talking about how the various systems work here, and some of those have been assembled into specific e-learning courses. That's the way in which we operate.

How do American schools and our education system compare with others around the world?

I think that when you talk about American schools, you're talking about great differences among schools in different parts of the country and even within the same city. Clearly there are American schools where people are coming out with the skills that are necessary to succeed, and clearly there are American schools where there's a lot of work still to be done to close the achievement gap. There are number of very talented researchers and dedicated people in schools who are trying to figure this out. I think they're making some progress.

There's a particular advancement at ETS called *cognitive-based assessment of, by, and for learning*. It looks at what the learning progressions are and how to measure how well someone is doing in mastering a particular learning progression so you can feed them, their teacher, and their family information and say, "Here's what you need to do next." Educational measurement is helping to get people more tools in this regard, but it's difficult. It's like the pit crew dilemma: How are you going to get the wheels off and the oil changed and get the car back in the race, because the school year moves on, kids get older. James Heckman out of Chicago has talked a great deal about putting more resources into early childhood [education]. I'm echoing a number of people in saying that putting more resources toward helping people develop in the first three years of life makes a huge difference in how they're going to perform in the educational world.

How do you measure and assess the outcomes of your learning goals?

There are at least three ways that we do that. When we take on a learning project, we go back to the work that the Robinsons did on gap analysis. We ask: Is this something that learning is going to make a difference on in the first place? Is this something that is really going to matter if we were to solve it? You have to ask those questions before you get into designing and implementing something.

The second way [particularly for leadership programs] is to ask whether those people have moved up in the organization? Been given greater accountability? Succeeded?

The third way is demand. If you're not getting people signing up for a session you've offered before, you need to take a look at that and say, "What's going on?" If you're getting more people signing up and the word of mouth is strong, that's important as well.

We're not big on smile sheets. We think that they are delivered too early and too simply. I don't think anybody can tell the value of a learning experience as they're walking out the door. That takes months for them to determine: Did I actually transfer what the activities brought forth for me?

Why is it important to really focus on building a learning organization?

If learning is about interpreting the world more effectively and the world keeps changing rapidly, then learning is the biggest boost that you have toward being successful. Otherwise you're just being swept along by events. An organization creates a business model within a particular opportunity space, and that space includes not only the environment but also what the competitors are doing, technological improvements, what people are discovering. All that is changing. We're carrying around smartphones that didn't exist a decade ago. We're dealing in an international environment that 10 years ago people were declaring, "Well, it's going to be peace forever," and it's anything but that. We've got climate issues. So if you're not able as an organization to figure out how you're going to interpret the world differently—in other words to learn—I don't think you're going to last very long.

What is key for the leaders of organizations to do to create this kind of learning culture?

Beware of confirmation bias. Question your assumptions. Have strategic conversations that engage many more viewpoints than they normally do in corporations. Engage what is referred to as the *wisdom of crowds*. That has to be balanced—don't turn it into a simple poll. But I think there are sources of information leaders need to take advantage of, especially looking at different age cohorts. What are your Millennials thinking about? Make sure to create diverse perspectives. Do you have underrepresented groups you're tapping into for leadership positions? Do you have gender balance? [Be sure that] you are not looking differently than the world looks when it comes to your leadership core or the people who are given responsibility for big projects.

Partial List of Chief Executive Officers, Chief Learning Officers, Chief Information Officers, Authors, and Thought Leaders Interviewed by Sarder TV

Good artists copy, great artists steal.

—Attributed to Pablo Picasso

We have interviewed more than 150 CEOs, CLOs, CIOs, learning experts, and leading thought leaders for Sarder TV, which we developed to help promote learning. Interviewees spoke with us on many of the key topics that we cover in this book, and we owe them a debt of gratitude—we could not have written the book without them. To hear their words for yourself, visit www.sarderTV.com.

Tracey Abbott, founder and CEO of Culture Relay; vice president of strategic planning at Foot Locker

Jennifer Alesia, global learning leader at General Electric; former head of learning and development at Mizuho Bank

David Allen, author of *Getting Things Done*

Samuel Bacharach, author of *Get Them on Your Side*, *Keep Them on Your Side*, and *When Charisma and Vision Are Not Enough*; professor at Cornell University

Robbie Baxter, author of *The Membership Economy*

Gary Beach, publisher emeritus of *CIO* magazine

Karin Bellantoni, president at BluePrint Sales Management Science (SMS)

Heather Bennett, VP of learning at ShoreTel

Megan Bilson, VP of global learning solutions of American Express

John Bowen, former CIO of PPL Corporation

Dick Brandt, director of the Iacocca Institute and Global Village Program

Mark Bunting, author of *Virtual Power*

Robert Burnside, CLO of Ketchum

Laurie Carey, CEO of We Connect the Dots

Talia Carner, author of *Hotel Moscow*

Janis Fisher Chan, author of *Designing and Developing Training Programs*, *Training Fundamentals*, and *E-Mail: A Write It Well Guide*

Savio Chan, CEO of US China Partners

Michael Chayes, managing principal of Sustained Leadership, LLC

Dorie Clark, author of *Stand Out*

Alison Cunard, general manager of Microsoft Learning Experiences (LeX)

Michael Cusumano, coauthor of *Strategy Rules*; professor at the Massachusetts Institute of Technology (MIT)

Susan Davis, founder, president, and CEO, BRAC USA

Jenny Dearborn, CLO of SAP

Dave DeFilippo, CLO of Suffolk Construction

Scott Delea, managing partner of Inflexion Interactive

Roseanna DeMaria, former CLO of Merrill Lynch; former CLO of New York University (NYU) School of Continuing and Professional Studies (SCPS)

Michael DeSimone, CEO of Borderfree

Ted Dinsmore, coauthor of *Partnering with Microsoft*

Russ Edelman, founder, president, and CEO of Corridor Company

Amy Edmondson, author of *Teaming*; professor at Harvard Business School

J.P. Eggers, associate professor at NYU Stern School of Business

T.J. Elliott, CLO of Educational Testing Service

Thomas (Tom) Evans, CLO of PricewaterhouseCoopers

Mark Fasciano, cofounder and managing director of Canrock Ventures; former CEO of FatWire Software

Keith Ferrazzi, CEO of Ferrazzi Greenlight; author of *Who's Got Your Back*

Ira Fuchs, Microsoft SharePoint technical specialist; author of *Enterprise Application Development in SharePoint 2010*

Jeff Furman, project management professional (PMP) instructor

Pankaj Ghemawat, author of *World 3.0: Global Prosperity and How to Achieve It*

William Green, author of *The Great Minds of Investing*

Susan Greenfield, author of *Mind Change*

Ranjay Gulati, coauthor of *Management*; professor at Harvard Business School

Danielle Harlan, founder and CEO of the Center for Advancing Leadership and Human Potential

Steve Heilenman, CIO of Computer Aid, Inc.

Rebecca Henderson, coeditor of *Leading Sustainable Change*; professor at Harvard Business School

David Hershfield, chief product officer of Auctionata

Edward (Ed) Hess, author of *Learn or Die* and *Growing an Entrepreneurial Business*; coeditor of *Leading with Values*; professor at the Darden School of Business

Linda Hill, coauthor of *Collective Genius*; professor at Harvard Business School

Dan Hoffman, former CEO of M5 Networks

Sheila Hooda, CEO and president of Alpha Advisory Partners

Thomas (Tom) Hyland, cofounder and partner, Aspada Investment Advisors

Michael (Mike) Indursky, president of Bliss World

Sukhbir Jasuja, cofounder and CEO of ITpreneurs

Jill Johnson, CEO of Workshop in Business Opportunities (WIBO) and Institute for Entrepreneurial Leadership (IFEL)

Karen Kang, author of *BrandingPays*; founder and CEO of BrandingPays, LLC

Rosabeth Moss Kanter, author of *Move*; professor at Harvard Business School

John Kauffman, business consultant and investor

Piper Kerman, author of *Orange Is the New Black*

Karen Kocher, CLO of Cigna

Arthur Langer, professor at Columbia University

Michelle Tillis Lederman, author of *Nail the Interview—Land the Job*

Daniel Leidl, director of organizational development and human capital at Production Resource Group (PRG)

Charlene Li, author of *The Engaged Leader*; founder and CEO of Altimeter Group

Steve Lohr, author of *Data-ism*; reporter at the *New York Times*

Michael Marquardt, author of *Leading with Questions*, *Optimizing the Power of Action Learning*, and *Building the Learning Organization*; professor at George Washington University

Michael Mauboussin, author of *The Success Equation*, *Think Twice*, and *More Than You Know*; professor of finance at Columbia Business School; managing director and head of global financial strategies at Credit Suisse

Bailey McCann, author of *Tactical Portfolios*

Jim McCann, CEO of 1-800-FLOWERS.COM

Rita Gunther McGrath, author of *The End of Competitive Advantage*; coauthor of *Discovery-Driven Growth* and *The Entrepreneurial Mindset*; professor at Columbia Business School

Ed McLaughlin, author of *The Purpose Is Profit*

Stephen Meister, author of *Commercial Real Estate Restructuring Revolution*; attorney and businessman

Daniel Meyer, CLO of Academica Virtual Education, LLC

Ben Michaelis, author of *Your Next Big Thing*

Bertrand Moingeon, coeditor of *Corporate and Organizational Identities* and *Organizational Learning and Competitive Advantage*; professor at HEC Paris

Robin Morgan, author of *Sisterhood Is Forever*, *Fighting Words*, and *The Burning Time*; poet; former child actor

Ira Neimark, author of *The Rise of Fashion and Lessons Learned at Bergdorf Goodman* and *Crossing Fifth Avenue to Bergdorf Goodman*; former CEO, Bergdorf Goodman

Valerie Norton, VP of talent management, Broadridge Financial Solutions, Inc.

Henry (Hank) Paulson, former U.S. secretary of the Treasury and CEO of Goldman Sachs

Rajendra Pawar, chairman and cofounder of NIIT

Mark Peterson, president of ctc TrainCanada

Ramona Pierson, cofounder and CEO of Declara

Sajan Pillai, CEO of UST Global

Linda Popky, author of *Marketing above the Noise: Achieve Strategic Advantage with Marketing That Matters*

Deborah Quazzo, founder and managing partner of Global Silicon Valley Advisors

Harish Rao, CEO of Interpersonal Frequency

Ken Rees, CEO of Elevate

Robert Reiss, coauthor of *The Transformative CEO*

Atefeh (Atti) Riazi, CIO of the United Nations

David Rose, author of *Angel Investing*; CEO of Gust

Bill Rosenthal, CEO, Communispond and Logical Operations

Maria Ross, author of *Branding Basics for Small Business*

Linda Rottenberg, author of *Crazy Is a Compliment*; CEO of Endeavor

Anand Sanwal, CEO and cofounder of CB Insights

Mohanbir (Mohan) Sawhney, coauthor of *Fewer, Bigger, Bolder: From Mindless Expansion to Focused Growth*; professor at Kellogg School of Management

Lewis Schiff, author of *Business Brilliant*

Alan Schnurman, former host of Lawline

David Schnurman, CEO of FurtherEd and Lawline

Gillian Zoe Segal, author of *Getting There*

Kabir Sehgal, author of *Coined*

Peter Senge, author of *The Fifth Discipline*; professor at MIT

Hindol Sengupta, editor-at-large at *Fortune India*

Richard Siemer, former CIO of NYC Human Resources Administration

Paul Silva, Microsoft technical architect, consultant, and educator

Russell Stevens, partner, Saddle River Group

Nick Stuart, CEO of Odyssey Networks; TV producer and journalist

Vincent Suppa, global human resources executive; adjunct professor at NYU

Wendy Suzuki, author of *Healthy Brain, Happy Life*

Joseph J. Tufano, VP and CIO of information technology of St. John's University

Michael Tull, author of *The Triangle Strategy*

Rachel Tuller, CEO and business coach of Vistage

NV "Tiger" Tyagarajan, president and CEO of Genpact

R "Ray" Wang, CEO of Constellation Research; author of *Disrupting Digital Business*

Brian Watson, coauthor of *Confessions of a Successful CIO*; former editor in chief of *CIO Insight*

Phil Weinzimer, author of *The Strategic CIO*; president of Strategere Consulting

Andrew Winston, author of *The Big Pivot* and *Green Recovery*; coauthor of *Green to Gold*

David Yoffie, coauthor of *Strategy Rules*; professor at Harvard Business School

Notes

Preface

1. "Henry Ford Quotes." BrainyQuote. Accessed August 21, 2015. http://www.brainyquote.com/quotes/quotes/h/henryford103927.html.
2. "What Made You Successful?" By Russell Sarder. Sarder TV video, 1:10. July 1, 2014. http://sardertv.com/made-successful-hank-paulson.
3. "Why Teens Are Impulsive, Addiction-Prone and Should Protect Their Brains." *Fresh Air*, NPR video, 38:12. January 28, 2015. http://www.npr.org/sections/health-shots/2015/01/28/381622350/why-teens-are-impulsive-addiction-prone-and-should-protect-their-brains.
4. "Why Building Learning Organization?" By Russell Sarder. Sarder TV video, 6:15. April 20, 2013. http://sardertv.com/building-learning-organization.

Chapter 1

1. Garvin, David A., Amy C. Edmondson, and Francesca Gino. "Is Yours a Learning Organization?" *Harvard Business Review*, March 2008. Accessed August 20, 2015. https://hbr.org/2008/03/is-yours-a-learning-organization/ar/1, emphasis in original.
2. Nicas, Jack, and Greg Bensinger. "The Delivery Drone Dilemma." *Wall Street Journal*, March 21, 2015, Weekend edition, B1.
3. "Bill Gates Quotes." BrainyQuote. Accessed August 20, 2015. http://www.brainyquote.com/quotes/quotes/b/billgates173262.html.
4. Mander, Jason. *GWI Social—Q4 2014*. January 21, 2015. Accessed August 20, 2015. http://www.slideshare.net/globalwebindex/gwi-social-report-q4-2014.
5. Clark, Don. "'Internet of Things' in Reach: Companies Rush into Devices Like Smart Door Locks, Appliances, but Limitations Exist."

Wall Street Journal, January 5, 2014. Accessed August 20, 2015. http://www.wsj.com/articles/SB10001424052702303640604579296580892973 264.

6. Dolan, Brian. "Fitbit Files for IPO, Sold Nearly 11 Million Fitness Devices in 2014." *MobiHealthNews*, May 7, 2015. Accessed August 20, 2015. http://mobihealthnews.com/43412/fitbit-files-for-ipo-sold-nearly-11-million-fitness-devices-in-2014.

7. Parker, Paisley. "The 'Internet of Things' Quotes to Consider." *Recurring Revenue Blog*, August 18, 2014. Accessed August 20, 2015. http://www.ariasystems.com/blog/internet-things-quotes-consider.

8. Molitch-Hiu, Michael. "Hod Lipson, 3D Printing, and the Fourth Industrial Revolution." 3D Printing Industry. April 29, 2015. Accessed August 20, 2015. http://3dprintingindustry.com/2015/04/29/hod-lipson-3d-printing-and-the-fourth-industrial-revolution.

9. SAS Institute. "Big Data: What It Is & Why It Matters." Accessed September 16, 2015. http://www.sas.com/en_us/insights/big-data/what-is-big-data.html.

10. Siegler, MG. "Eric Schmidt: Every 2 Days We Create as Much Information as We Did up to 2003." TechCrunch. August 4, 2010. Accessed August 20, 2015. http://techcrunch.com/2010/08/04/schmidt-data.

11. Microsoft. "Satya Nadella email to employees on first day as CEO." News release, February 4, 2014. Accessed August 20, 2015. http://news.microsoft.com/2014/02/04/satya-nadella-email-to-employees-on-first-day-as-ceo.

12. Sanders, Sam. "Whole Foods Tries to Shake 'Whole Paycheck' Rep with Cheaper Spinoff." *The Salt*, NPR. May 8, 2015. Accessed August 20, 2015. http://www.npr.org/sections/thesalt/2015/05/08/405125477/whole-foods-to-open-chain-of-lower-priced-stores.

13. Microsoft. "Microsoft Empowers Windows, IOS, Android, Mac and Linux Developers to Reach Billions of New Customers." News release, April 29, 2015. http://news.microsoft.com/2015/04/29/microsoft-empowers-windows-ios-android-mac-and-linux-developers-to-reach-billions-of-new-customers.

14. *Wikipedia*, s.v. "Microsoft Mobile." Last modified September 16, 2015. Accessed September 16, 2015. https://en.wikipedia.org/wiki/Microsoft_Mobile.

15. "Jack Welch Quotes." BrainyQuote. Accessed August 20, 2015. http://www.brainyquote.com/quotes/quotes/j/jackwelch163678.html.

16. "Why Invest in Employee Training & Development?" By Russell Sarder. Sarder TV video, 1:38. November 7, 2013. http://sardertv.com/invest-employee-training-development-rachel-tuller-coach-consultant-vistage.

17. Galagan, Pat. "Bridging the Skills Gap Part I." *The Public Manager*, October 23, 2009. Accessed August 20, 2015. https://www.td .org/Publications/Magazines/The-Public-Manager/Archives/2009/10/ Bridging-the-Skills-Gap-Part-I.

18. U.S. Bureau of Labor Statistics. "Labor Force Statistics from the Current Population Survey." Accessed August 20, 2015. http://data.bls.gov/ timeseries/LNS14000000.

19. Robert Half Technology. *2012 Salary Guide: Technology Salary and Hiring Trends*. Accessed August 20, 2015. https://www.sc.edu/career/Pdf/ RH_TechSalaries.pdf.

20. Deloitte. *Global Human Capital Trends 2014*. Accessed August 20, 2015. http://www2.deloitte.com/sa/en/pages/human-capital/articles/human-capital-trends-2014.html.

21. GE Capital. *Learning by Doing: GE's Approach to Developing People*. 2012. Accessed August 20, 2015. http://www.gecapital.com/en/pdf/GE_Capital_ Example_Learning_By_Doing.pdf.

22. Bersin, Josh. *The Corporate Learning Factbook 2014*. "Spending on Corporate Training Soars: Employee Capabilities Now a Priority." *Forbes*, February 4, 2014. Accessed August 20, 2015. http://www.forbes .com/sites/joshbersin/2014/02/04/the-recovery-arrives-corporate-training-spend-skyrockets.

23. Leung, Rebecca. "Jack Welch: 'I Fell In Love.'" *60 Minutes*, March 25, 2005. Accessed August 20, 2015. http://www.cbsnews.com/news/jack-welch-i-fell-in-love.

24. *Merriam-Webster Online*, s.v. "learning." Accessed August 20, 2015. http://www.merriam-webster.com/dictionary/learning.

25. Senge, Peter M. *The Fifth Discipline: The Art & Practice of the Learning Organization*. Rev. ed. New York: Doubleday/Currency, 2006.

26. *Dictionary.com*, s.v. "culture." Accessed September 17, 2015. http:// dictionary.reference.com/browse/culture.

27. Kouzes, James M., and Barry Z. Posner. *The Leadership Challenge*. 4th ed. San Francisco: Jossey-Bass, 2007, italics in original.

28. Kanter, Rosabeth Moss. "Ten Reasons People Resist Change." *Harvard Business Review*, September 25, 2012. Accessed August 20, 2015. https:// hbr.org/2012/09/ten-reasons-people-resist-change.

Chapter 2

1. Marquardt, Michael J. *Building the Learning Organization: Achieving Strategic Advantage through a Commitment to Learning*. 3rd ed. Boston: Nicholas Brealey, 2011.

2. "Turkish Language, Culture, Customs and Etiquette." Kwintessential. Accessed August 20, 2015. http://www.kwintessential.co.uk/resources/ global-etiquette/turkey-country-profile.html.

3. Herb Kelleher, chairman Emeritus and former CEO of Southwest Airlines, quoted in Andy Hanselman. "What's Culture—and What's Yours?" Management-Issues.com. July 2013. Accessed August 20, 2015. http:// www.management-issues.com/opinion/6719/whats-culture-and-whats-yours.

4. Senge, Peter M. *The Fifth Discipline: The Art & Practice of the Learning Organization.* Rev. ed. New York: Doubleday/Currency, 2006.

5. *Dictionary.com*, s.v. "leader." Accessed August 20, 2015. http://dictionary. reference.com/browse/leader.

6. Kouzes, James M., and Barry Z. Posner. *The Leadership Challenge.* 4th ed. San Francisco: Jossey-Bass, 2007.

7. Marquardt, *Building the Learning Organization*, 216.

8. Kouzes and Posner, *Leadership Challenge*, 17.

9. Conant, Douglas, and Mette Norgaard. *TouchPoints: Creating Powerful Leadership Connections in the Smallest of Moments.* San Francisco: Jossey-Bass, 2011.

10. Marquardt, *Building the Learning Organization*, 216.

11. Kouzes and Posner, *Leadership Challenge*, 15, emphasis added.

12. Hess, Edward D. Introduction to *Learn or Die: Using Science to Build a Leading-Edge Learning Organization.* New York: Columbia University Press, 2014.

13. Kouzes and Posner, *Leadership Challenge*, 199.

14. "How to Build Team Culture?" By Russell Sarder. Sarder TV video, 1:10. November 13, 2012. Accessed August 20, 2015. http://sardertv .com/hiring-lessons.

Chapter 3

1. "Richard C. Cushing on Planning." QuotationsBook.com. Accessed August 20, 2015. http://quotationsbook.com/quote/30460.

2. "Alan Lakein Quotes." BrainyQuote. Accessed August 20, 2015. http:// www.brainyquote.com/quotes/quotes/a/alanlakein154655.html.

3. Hess, Edward D. *Learn or Die: Using Science to Build a Leading-Edge Learning Organization.* New York: Columbia University Press, 2014.

4. Padgaonkar, Abhay. "Size Matters: Smaller Project Teams Are Better." InformationWeek. May 2, 2013. http://www.informationweek.com/it-leadership/size-matters-smaller-project-teams-are-better/d/d-id/1109788.

5. Gupta, Kavita, Catherine M. Sleezer, and Darlene F. Russ-Eft. *A Practical Guide to Needs Assessment.* 2nd ed. San Francisco: Pfeiffer, 2007.
6. Gupta, Sleezer, and Russ-Eft, *Practical Guide*, 16.
7. Klaus Wittkuhns, senior vice president of people operations for Google, quoted in Harold Jarche. *Workplace Performance Analysis.* Accessed August 20, 2015. http://www.jarche.com/wp-content/uploads/2007/06/jarche_analysis_process.pdf.

Chapter 4

1. Oracle. *Goal Setting: A Fresh Perspective.* June 2012. http://www.oracle.com/us/media1/goal-setting-fresh-perspective-ee-1679275.pdf.
2. Oracle, *Goal Setting*, 3.
3. Doran, George T. "There's a S.M.A.R.T. Way to Write Management's Goals and Objectives." *Management Review* 70, no. 11 (1981): 35–36.
4. Csikszentmihalyi, Mihaly. *Flow: The Psychology of Optimal Experience.* New York: Harper & Row, 1990.
5. Locke, Edwin A., and Gary P. Latham. *A Theory of Goal Setting & Task Performance.* Englewood Cliffs, NJ: Prentice Hall, 1990.
6. Latham, Gary P., and Gerard Seijts. "Learning Goals or Performance Goals: Is It the Journey or the Destination?" *Ivey Business Journal*, May/June 2006. http://iveybusinessjournal.com/publication/learning-goals-or-performance-goals-is-it-the-journey-or-the-destination.
7. Hewlett, Sylvia Ann, and Carolyn Buck Luce. "Extreme Jobs: The Dangerous Allure of the 70-Hour Workweek." *Harvard Business Review*, December 2006. https://hbr.org/2006/12/extreme-jobs-the-dangerous-allure-of-the-70-hour-workweek/ar/1.

Chapter 5

1. Noonan, Melissa. "Competency Models—What Are They Anyhow and What's the Big Deal?" *St. Charles Consulting Group* 27 (June 2012). http://www.stccg.com/competency-models-what-are-they.
2. Laszlo Bock quoted in Thomas L. Friedman "How to Get a Job at Google." *New York Times*, February 22, 2014. http://www.nytimes.com/2014/02/23/opinion/sunday/friedman-how-to-get-a-job-at-google.html?_r=1.
3. Gupta, Kavita, Catherine M. Sleezer, and Darlene F. Russ-Eft. *A Practical Guide to Needs Assessment.* 2nd ed. San Francisco: Pfeiffer, 2007.

4. McClelland, David C. "Testing for Competence Rather Than for 'Intelligence.'" *American Psychologist* 28, no. 1 (January 1973): 1–14.

5. Clark, Donald. "Bloom's Taxonomy of Learning Domains." Big Dog & Little Dog's Performance Juxtaposition. Last modified January 12, 2015. http://www.nwlink.com/~donclark/hrd/bloom.html.

6. "That Alvin Toffler Quotation." *Flexnib* (blog), July 3, 2013. http://www.flexnib.com/2013/07/03/that-alvin-toffler-quotation.

7. Fisch, Karl, and Scott McLeod. "Did You Know; Shift Happens— Globalization; Information Age." YouTube video, 6:07. Last modified February 8, 2007. https://www.youtube.com/watch?v=ljbI-363A2Q.

8. Davies, Anna, Devin Fidler, and Marina Gorbis. *Future Work Skills 2020.* Institute for the Future for the University of Phoenix Research Institute 2011. Accessed September 18, 2015. http://www.iftf.org/futureworkskills.

9. Institute for the Future for the University of Phoenix Research Institute Partnership for 21st Century Learning. "P21 Releases Framework for State Action on Global Education Framework." News release, September 10, 2010. http://www.p21.org/news-events/press-releases/1495-p21-releases-framework-for-state-action-on-global-education-framework.

10. Orr, J. Evelyn, Craig Sneltjes, and Guangrong Dai. *The Art and Science of Competency Modeling: Best Practices in Developing and Implementing Success Profiles.* Korn/Ferry Institute white paper 2010. Accessed August 20, 2015. http://www.kornferry.com/media/lominger_pdf/Final_CompMdling_web_2.pdf.

11. Mansfield, Richard S. *Practical Questions in Building Competency Models.* 2005. Accessed August 20, 2015. https://www.lexonis.com/resources/practical%20questions%20building%20models.pdf.

12. In an interview with Savio Chan, chief executive officer at U.S. China Partners and president of U.S. Pan Asian American Chamber of Commerce, "How to Find the Right People?" Sarder TV. 3:55. November 17, 2012. https://www.youtube.com/watch?v=KoZL2tFGOWk.

13. Gupta, Sleezer, and Russ-Eft, *Practical Guide*, 15.

14. McNamara, Carter. "Assessing Your Training Needs: Needs Assessment to Training Goals." Free Management Library. Accessed August 20, 2015. http://managementhelp.org/training/systematic/needs-assessment.htm.

Chapter 6

1. "Bill Gates Quotes." Accessed September 18, 2015. http://www.inspirationalstories.com/quotes/bill-gates-we-all-learn-best-in-our-own.

2. Sarder, Russell. *Effective Learning Methods: How to Develop the Most Effective Learning Method.* New York: Sarder Press, 2011.

3. *Training* staff. "2013 Training Industry Report." *Training*, November/December 2013. http://www.trainingmag.com/2013-training-industry-report.

4. In an interview with Jennifer Alesia, global learning leader at General Electric (GE), "What Is the Most Effective Learning Plan?" Sarder TV video, 1:38. June 7, 2014. http://sardertv.com/effective-learning-plan.

5. "In His Own Words: Quotes by Lombardi." ESPN Classic. Accessed August 20, 2015. http://espn.go.com/classic/quotes_Lombardi.html.

6. In an interview with Lewis Schiff, executive director of *Inc.* magazine's Business Owners Council and author of *Business Brilliant*, "Do You Have a Mentor?" Sarder TV video, 3:32. August 29, 2013. http://sardertv.com/do-you-have-a-mentor.

7. *Oxford Essential Quotations*, s.v. "Aristotle 384–322 BC." Accessed August 20, 2015. http://www.oxfordreference.com/view/10.1093/acref/9780191735240.001.0001/q-oro-00000434.

8. Gladwell, Malcolm. *Blink: The Power of Thinking without Thinking*. New York: Back Bay Books, 2007.

9. U.S. Department of Labor. "Apprenticeship." Accessed August 20, 2015. http://www.dol.gov/dol/topic/training/apprenticeship.htm.

10. Kumon. "The Importance of Self-Learning." Accessed August 20, 2015. http://www.kumon.com/resources/the-importance-of-self-learning.

11. "Aldous Huxley Quotes." BrainyQuote. Accessed August 20, 2015. http://www.brainyquote.com/quotes/quotes/a/aldoushux122020.html.

12. In an interview with Heather Bennett, vice president of learning at ShoreTel, "What Is the Most Effective Learning Method?" By Russell Sarder. Sarder TV video, 2:11. February 20, 2013. http://sardertv.com/what-is-the-most-effective-learning-method-heather.

13. Gray, Caroline. "Blended Learning: Why Everything Old Is New Again—but Better." *ATD Links*, February 15, 2006. https://www.td.org/Publications/Newsletters/Links/2006/02/Blended-Learning-Why-Everything-Old-Is-New-Again-but-Better.

14. In an interview with Laurie Carey, chief executive officer of We Connect the Dots, "What Is the Most Effective Learning Method?" Sarder TV video, 4:56. November 12, 2013. http://sardertv.com/effective-learning-method-laurie-carey-ceo-connect-dots/.

15. In an interview with Peter Senge, "Define 'Learning.'" Sarder TV. Accessed August 20, 2015. http://www.russellsarder.com/define-learning.

16. Gladwell, Malcolm. *Outliers: The Story of Success*. New York: Little, Brown and Company, 2008.

Chapter 7

1. Hodell, Chuck. *ISD from the Ground Up: A No-Nonsense Approach to Instructional Design.* 2nd ed. Alexandria, VA: ASTD Press, 2006.

2. Preskill, Hallie, and Katelyn Mack. *Building a Strategic Learning and Evaluation System for Your Organization.* Accessed August 20, 2015. http://flanagan-hyde.com/wp-content/uploads/2015/06/Building_an_Evaluation_System.pdf.

3. In an interview with Jeff Furman, NetCom Learning instructor and author of *The Project Management Answer Book.* "How to Measure ROI for Employee Training?" Sarder TV video, 1:52. October 25, 2012. http://sardertv.com/how-to-measure-roi-for-employee-training.

4. In an interview with Michael Tull, adjunct professor at New York University and author of *The Triangle Strategy*, "How to Measure Training ROI?" Sarder TV video, 2:40. August 9, 2013. http://sardertv.com/how-to-measure-training-roi-3.

5. In an interview with Jeff Furman, NetCom Learning instructor and author of *The Project Management Answer Book*, "How to Measure ROI for Employee Training?" Sarder TV video, 1:52. October 25, 2012. http://sardertv.com/how-tomeasure-roi-for-employee-training.

Chapter 8

1. "Jack Welch Quotes." BrainyQuote. Accessed August 20, 2015. http://www.brainyquote.com/quotes/authors/j/jack_welch.html.

2. Francis, David R. "Why Companies Pay for College." National Bureau of Economic Research. Accessed September 19, 2015. http://www.nber.org/digest/feb03/w9225.html.

3. National Association of Colleges and Employers. *The Class of 2011 Student Survey Report.* Bethlehem, PA: National Association of Colleges and Employers, September 2011.

4. Ellis, Ryann K. *A Field Guide to Learning Management Systems.* 2009. www.astd.org/~/media/Files/Publications/LMS_fieldguide_20091.

5. MarketsandMarkets. "Learning Management Systems (LMS) Market Worth $7.83 Billion by 2018 Forecasted in MarketsandMarkets Recent Report." News release, October 29, 2013. http://www.marketwired.com/press-release/learning-management-systems-lms-market-worth-783-billion-2018-forecasted-marketsandmarkets-1845977.htm.

6. Sleight, Deborah Alpert. "What Is Electronic Performance Support and What Isn't?" 1993. Accessed August 20, 2015. https://www.msu.edu/~sleightd/epssyn.html.

Chapter 9

1. Zhiwen, Yu. "No Retirement from Learning—OUC's 90-Year-Old Lu Juzhong Honored with Graduation Certificate." Open University of China. December 2014. http://en.ouchn.edu.cn/index.php/news-109/campus/1438-no-retirement-from-learning-ouc-s-90-year-old-.
2. "Bill Gates Quotes." BrainyQuote. Accessed August 20, 2015. http://www.brainyquote.com/quotes/quotes/b/billgates626259.html.
3. Miller, Claire Cain. "As Robots Grow Smarter, American Workers Struggle to Keep Up." *New York Times*, December 15, 2014. http://www.nytimes.com/2014/12/16/upshot/as-robots-grow-smarter-american-workers-struggle-to-keep-up.html?_r=0&abt=0002&abg=1.
4. Hamel, Liz, Jamie Firth, and Mollyann Brodie. "Kaiser Family Foundation/New York Times/CBS News Non-Employed Poll." Kaiser Family Foundation. December 11, 2014. http://kff.org/other/poll-finding/kaiser-family-foundationnew-york-timescbs-news-non-employed-poll.
5. Miller, "As Robots Grow Smarter."
6. Anthony J. D'Angelo, quoted in Sarder, Russell. *Learning: Steps to Becoming a Passionate Lifelong Learner*. New York: Sarder Press, 2011.
7. In an interview with Laurie Carey, "Learning is Neuroplasticity," Sarder TV video, 6:21, November 12, 2013. http://sardertv.com/laurie-carey-ceo-connect-dots.
8. Hess, Edward D. *Learn or Die: Using Science to Build a Leading-Edge Learning Organization*. New York: Columbia University Press, 2014.
9. Peter Drucker quoted in Rubin, Harriet. "Peter's Principles." *Inc.*, March 1, 1998. http://www.inc.com/magazine/19980301/887.html.
10. B.B. King quoted in Sarder, Russell. *Learning: Steps to Becoming a Passionate Lifelong Learner*. New York: Sarder Press, 2011, 35.
11. Conant, Douglas, and Mette Norgaard. *TouchPoints: Creating Powerful Leadership Connections in the Smallest of Moments*. San Francisco: Jossey-Bass, 2011.
12. Lesinski, Jeanne M. *Bill Gates: Entrepreneur and Philanthropist*. Lifeline Biographies. Minneapolis: Twenty-First Century Books, 2008.
13. Moore, Peter. "Poll Results: Reading." YouGov: September 30, 2013. https://today.yougov.com/news/2013/09/30/poll-results-reading.
14. Rainie, Lee, and Maeve Duggan. "E-book Reading Jumps; Print Book Reading Declines." Pew Research Center. December 27, 2012. http://libraries.pewinternet.org/2012/12/27/e-book-reading-jumps-print-book-reading-declines.

15. Flippo, Hyde. "German Myth 12: The Famous 'Goethe' Quotation." About.com German Language. Accessed August 20, 2015. http:// german.about.com/library/blgermyth12.htm.

16. "Mahatma Gandhi Quotes." BrainyQuote. Accessed August 20, 2015. http:// www.brainyquote.com/quotes/quotes/m/mahatmagan109075.html.

17. Nelson Mandela quoted in United Nations. "Education for All (EFA)." Accessed August 20, 2015. http://www.un.org/en/globalissues/ briefingpapers/efa/quotes.shtml.

18. Federal News Service. "Barack Obama's Feb. 5 Speech." *New York Times*, February 5, 2008. http://www.nytimes.com/2008/02/05/us/politics/ 05text-obama.html?pagewanted=print&_r=0&gwh=30999E9A982F7E A02C0215A84F1BB471&gwt=pay.

19. In an interview with Jill Johnson, cofounder/CEO of the Institute for Entrepreneurial Leadership and CEO of Workshop in Business Opportunities, "How to Improve U.S. Education System." Sarder TV video, 4:30. June 26, 2014. http://sardertv.com/improve-u-s-education-system.

20. Clay Bedford quoted in Callahan, Dennis. "50 Quotes about Learning." *Learnstreaming* (blog), May 16, 2011. Accessed August 20, 2015. http:// learnstreaming.com/50-quotes-about-learning.

21. Hess, *Learn or Die*, 47.

22. Organization for Economic Cooperation and Development. "Indicator A2 How Many Students Are Expected to Complete Upper Secondary Education?" In *Education at a Glance 2014: OECD Indicators*, 54–73. Accessed August 20, 2015. doi:10.1787/eag-2014-7-en.

23. Partnership for 21st Century Learning. "P21 Releases Framework for State Action on Global Education Framework." News release, September 10, 2010. http://www.p21.org/news-events/press-releases/1495-p21- releases-framework-for-state-action-on-global-education-framework.

24. Center for Children & Technology. "Publications: Assessment of 21st Century Skills: The Current Landscape." June 1, 2005. http://cct.edc .org/publications/assessment-21st-century-skills-current-landscape.

25. Partnership for 21st Century letter to Tom Harkin and Jerry Moran, June 2, 2014. Accessed August 21, 2015. www.p21.org/storage/ documents/docs/P21_FY15_Budget_Letter_Senate_Final.pdf.

26. Huntsberry, William. "Meet the Classroom of the Future." NPR Ed. January 12, 2015. http://www.npr.org/sections/ed/2015/01/12/370966699/meet- the-classroom-of-the-future.

27. Kevin Carey, director of the Education Policy Program at the New America Foundation, quoted in "Prepare for 'The End of College': Here's What Free Higher Ed Looks Like." By Terry Gross. NPR Ed. March 3, 2015. http://www.npr.org/sections/ed/2015/03/03/390167950/ prepare-for-the-end-of-college-heres-what-free-higher-ed-looks-like.

Learning from Experts: Excerpts From Sarder TV Interviews

1. Society for Organizational Learning North America. "About SoL North America." Accessed September 21, 2015. www.solonline.org/?page= AboutSoL.

References and Resources

References

Argyris, Chris. *Knowledge for Action: A Guide to Overcoming Barriers to Organizational Flawed Change*. San Francisco: Jossey-Bass, 1993.

———. *Flawed Advice and the Management Trap: How Managers Can Know When They're Getting Good Advice and When They're Not*. New York: Oxford University Press, 2000.

Bloom, Benjamin S. *Taxonomy of Educational Objectives*. Boston: Allyn and Bacon, 1984.

Caffarella, Rosemary S., and Sandra Ratcliff Daffron. *Planning Programs for Adult Learners: A Practical Guide*. San Francisco: Jossey-Bass, 2001.

Carey, Kevin. *The End of College: Creating the Future of Learning and the University of Everywhere*. New York: Riverhead Books, 2015.

Chan, Janis Fisher. *Designing and Developing Training Programs*. Pfeiffer Essential Guides to Training Basics. San Francisco: Pfeiffer, 2010.

Conant, Douglas R., and Mette Norgaard. *TouchPoints: Creating Powerful Leadership Connections in the Smallest of Moments*. San Francisco: Jossey-Bass, 2011.

Conley, Chip. *Peak: How Great Companies Get Their Mojo from Maslow*. San Francisco: Jossey-Bass, 2007.

Cummings, Thomas G., ed. *Handbook of Organization Development*. Los Angeles: Sage Publications, 2008.

Gupta, Kavita, Catherine M. Sleezer, and Darlene F. Russ-Eft. *A Practical Guide to Needs Assessment*. 2nd ed. San Francisco: Pfeiffer, 2007.

Hess, Edward D. *Learn or Die: Using Science to Build a Leading-Edge Learning Organization*. New York: Columbia University Press, 2014.

Hodell, Chuck. *ISD from the Ground Up: A No-Nonsense Approach to Instructional Design*. 2nd ed. Alexandria, VA: ASTD Press, 2006.

Kirkpatrick, Donald L., and James D. Kirkpatrick. *Evaluating Training Programs: The Four Levels*. 3rd ed. San Francisco: Berrett-Koehler, 2006.

Kouzes, James M., and Barry Z. Posner. *The Leadership Challenge Workshop, Intro Participant Set*. San Francisco: Jossey-Bass, 2010.

Krames, Jeffrey A. *What the Best CEOs Know: 7 Exceptional Leaders and Their Lessons for Transforming Any Business*. New York: McGraw-Hill, 2005.

Locke, Edwin A., and Gary P. Latham. *A Theory of Goal Setting & Task Performance*. Englewood Cliffs, NJ: Prentice Hall, 1990.

Mager, Robert F. *Preparing Instructional Objectives: A Critical Tool in the Development of Effective Instruction*. 3rd ed. Atlanta, GA: Center for Effective Performance, 1997.

Marquardt, Michael J. *Building the Learning Organization: Achieving Strategic Advantage through a Commitment to Learning*. 3rd ed. Boston: Nicholas Brealey, 2011.

Sarder, Russell. *Effective Learning Methods: How to Develop the Most Effective Learning Method*. New York: Sarder Press, 2011.

———. *Learning: Steps to Becoming a Passionate Lifelong Learner*. New York: Sarder Press, 2011.

Schein, Edgar H. *Organizational Culture and Leadership*. 4th ed. San Francisco: Jossey-Bass, 2010.

Senge, Peter M. *The Fifth Discipline Fieldbook: Strategies and Tools for Building a Learning Organization*. New York: Doubleday/Currency, 1994.

———. *The Fifth Discipline: The Art & Practice of the Learning Organization*. Rev. ed. New York: Doubleday/Currency, 2006.

Shani, A. B. (Rami), and Peter Docherty. *Learning by Design: Building Sustainable Organizations*. Management, Organizations, and Business. Malden, MA: Blackwell Publishing, 2003.

Stolovitch, Harold D., and Erica J. Keeps. *Telling Ain't Training*. Alexandria, VA: ASTD, 2002.

Wurtzel, Alan. L. *Good to Great to Gone: The 60 Year Rise and Fall of Circuit City*. New York: Diversion Books, 2012.

Useful Websites

American Management Association, www.amanet.org

Association for Talent Development (ATD, formerly called ASTD, American Society for Training & Development), www.td.org

Deloitte's Human Capital Services, http://www2.deloitte.com/global/en/services/human-capital.html

Harvard Business Review, https://hbr.org

Korn Ferry Institute, http://www.kornferry.com/institute

Oracle's best practices, https://www.oracle.com/applications/modern-best-practice/hr-and-talent-management

Society for Human Resource Management, www.shrm.org

Acknowledgments

To say that *Building an Innovative Learning Organization* is "by Russell Sarder" overstates the case. This book is the result of a team effort, not only during its writing, but also throughout my upbringing, education, and career. I always believed that a team with the best players usually wins, and I would like to acknowledge the many people who have been instrumental in bringing this book to life.

I could not have completed this book without the help of author, editor, trainer, and instructional designer **Janis Fisher Chan**. I have been a big fan of hers for many years, and it was an honor working with her. Thank you for helping me research, write, and edit the book and fine-tune my learning framework. You're a great teacher!

This book would not have been possible were it not for the efforts of **Tuan Yang** and her skills in people development, people management, strategy, and execution of strategy. Thank you, Yang, for putting together a great team and managing this project from beginning to end. I admire your creativity, your business acumen, and your ability to always get things done.

You are holding this book in your hands because of the efforts of my agent, **Jeff Herman** (http://www.jeffherman.com/), and my publisher, **John Wiley & Sons**, who understood its value and supported its publication. Thank you.

Jim Collins once said, "The most important decisions business people make are not 'what' decisions but 'who' decisions." I want sincerely to thank some of the **current and former employees** of NetCom Learning, Sarder TV, Learning CMS, and LearningGG who gave me the opportunity to learn from them:

Adam Farage, Adam Chng, Ady Chng, Ahm Rahman, Ahmed Kuhla, Alex Cornwell, Alex Martinez, Alexander Shick, Allan Jacobs, Allen Jenne, Alma L. Dewberry, Alok Singh, Alyssa Codamon, Amanda Teer, Amidz Zaman, Amit Kaw, Anand Dandapani, Andre Beache, Andrew Braun, Andrew McQuade, Andrew Wen, Andy Gaston, Andy Ramroop, Angelica Camacho, Angie Cunningham, Anita Hui Tu, Ankuna Gulati, Ankur Bhatt, Anthony Heyliger, Anthony Khan, Anthony Ribando, Anthony Rodriguez, Armani Rouse, Ashley Heyliger, Barry Geisler, Barry Tesser, Barry Zimmerman, Ben Cheng, Beridania Fernandez, Bill Boyette, Bill Kruk, Bill Malone, Blessy Torres, Bob Briller, Bobby Ceklic, Bobby Williams, Brad Parker, Bradley Dungca, Brian Ciufo, Brian P. Smith, Bruce Palmer, Candi Heyliger, Carl Schnedeker, Carlos Craig, Carmille Agana, Carolina Hanysz, Caroline Burbank, Chanel Carlos, Charles Williams, Chet DeFour, Chris Diego, Chris Martin, Chris Massimillo, Chuck Hayden, Chun Hui, Clay Shaw, Courtenay Gillean Cholovich, Craig Campbell, Cristian Palomino, Dallas Bird, Damian Laljie, Daniel Casillas, Daniel Greenspan, Daniel Gregory, Daniel Yun, Daphne Colon, Darrin Wilson, David Fremed, David Miller, Debra Cirillo, Deepali Sharma, Dennis Vu, Denzil Brown, Devin Gaston, DeWight Bridges, Diana Edwards, Dirk Anthony, Disha Kamra, Dmitriy Chumachenko, Edward Covell, Edward Franke, Edward Parker, Eileah Phinnessee, Elianna Neofotistos, Emilio Grande, Eric Bernstein, Eric Smith, Eugenia Bachaleda, Fea Ming Tang, Feven Woldu, Frances Faulkner, Frances Whisnant, Francisco Sotomayor, Frank Lopez, Frank Pisco, Fred V. Torres, Gabi Golan, Georgia Tsomos, Geraldine O'Donnell, Glen

Chambers, Grace Capra, Greg Massengale, Gregory Dama, Gregory Mosiejewski, Guy Hinson, Harmon Kennedy, Harris Jalil, Harry Schlereth, Harvey Joel Meyer, Hieu Tran, Holden Contreras, Houdini Owens, Ignacio Jimenez, Ilya Piyevsky, Ilya Vayser, Ilya Volovnik, Irene Falco, Irwan Gohor, Jacqueline Forbes-Clarke, Jaideep Nandy, Jaivie Robles, Jamar Blue, James Allen, James Mayer, Jane Natalie Aragon, Jasmine Marrero, Jason Kane, Jason Moss, Jason Salsiccia, Jay Chakroborty, Jeffrey Goldstein, Jemal Joseph, Jennifer Fang, Jenny Long, Jesse Nunez, Jessica Ventura, Jessica Weijola, Jiaqing Chen, Jim Buldo, Joanna Parigori, John Chan, John Giordano, John Molnar, John Montague III, John Watkins, Jong Lee, Jose Fernandez, Joseph Contello, Joseph P. Igana, Josh Jenner, Joshua Palmieri, Justin Friedman, Kalin Kirev, Kamal Kishore, Kamil Mansuri, Kandice Amir, Karthik Krishnan, Kate Luna, Kate Nickels, Kathline E. Surpris, Katie Jones, Keith Charles, Kelcey Gosserand, Kellin Bliss, Kenneth Foxton, Kevin Paredes, Kiana Sullivan, Kimberly Dillon, Kirsten M. Kallon, Krishna Maddipatla, Kristie Caballero, Kristin Meyer, Kristina Villarini, Kyle Mroz, Laura Caputo, Lawrence Mital, Leopold Momplaisir, Les Calloway, Lester Hernandez, Leticia Hanysz-Narvaez, Lira Cafe, Livingston Taylor, Lonnie Smith, Lou Bailey, Luis Segarra, Luis Vargas, Malika Lowe, Mamunur Rashid, Manish Kalani, Manzur A. Mazumder, Marcelo Cornieles, Margaret Haymann, Maria Bata, Maria Tsampounieri, Maria Waksmunski, Mario Romero, Marion Martinelli, Marlon Jones-Guma, Marvin Rucker, Mary Dama, Mary Ellen de Jesus, Mary Rose Feeney, Masako Masuda, Masud Rahman, Matthew Halvorsen, Maurice Murry, Meeran Saxena, Megan Haney, Mel Tabari, Melissa Davis, Michael Amponin, Michael Baird, Michael Chan, Michael Govinda, Michael Grossman, Michael Hudak, Michael Justin, Michael Patterson, Michael Shkolnik, Michael Valdes, Michael Zachensky, Michele DeChaine, Michelle Casillas, Mike Ferry,

Mingming Dong, Minni Chawla, Mitchell Silverman, Mizanur Kazi, Mohammad Rahman, Monica Cummings, Monica Perlas, Monique Clini, Monique Contreras, Monique Murray, Morris Brown, Mudit Mittal, Munasir Choudhury, Mustafa Er, Nancy Manzar, Nancy Mora, Natalie Pecora, Naushad Hasan, Naveen Bhutani, Neal Otter, Neil Masih, Niamh Switzer, Nicholas Ntovas, Nicholas Tognazzi, Nora Sevillano, Nusrat Hossain, Nusrath Ananna, Octavia Jordan, Olisa Christian, Oscar Peña, Patrice Haith, Patrick Altema, Patrick Ferrante, Patrick Robison, Paul Pollikoff, Paul Siegel, Paul Silva, Paul Vandeyar, Paulson Ambookan, Phil Cincotta, Phil Guerra, Phillip Kyaw, Praveen Shrivastava, Preeti Kachroo, Qing Yang Gao, Rachel Hunt, Ramesh Periasamy, Ray Rohoman, Raymond Bernard, Reynel Santiago, Rhiannon Molina, Richard Brown, Richard Landrigan, Rinchen Khampa, Ritesh Jha, River Xin, Robby Manubay, Robert Hardy, Robert Holmes, Robert Kratzke, Robert Sharron, Roberto Rodriguez, Robin Cunningham, Ronald Fayziyev, Ronnette Griffin, Ronnie Green, Rosangeli Arce, Rosemary Perez, Rubel Khan, Ruchi Goyal, Ruchi Singh, Rui Zhang, Rumman Prodhan, Ryan Dunlap, Saira Jabbar, Sally Yin, Samantha Warden, Samuel Denny, Sandra Lemon, Sanjeev Agarwal, Sanjeev Shrivastava, Sarah Bowling, Sarah Hedeen, Sayed Jamil, Sean Oriyano, Sean Park, Sharon Chen, Shelly Owens, Sherry Wang, Shweta Dharmadhikari, Snehasish Halder, Stacey Wright, Steve Magoon, Steve Wexler, Steven Lefstein, Steven Padilla, Stuart Katzanek, Sunita Crasto, Sunny Khan, Sunny Sharma, Susan Koyfman, Susan Rodriguez, Tamanna Chowdhury, Therese Switzer, Thomas Cox, Thomas Gocke, Tiara Tang, Tiffany Cureau, Tim Driscoll, Tina Thompson, Titu Sarder, Tom Spisso, Tony Yao, Tracy Waffenfeld, Tuan Yang, Tyrone McQueen, Uma Sharma, Umar Khitab, Valerie Gonzalez, Vanessa Tisdale, Vanita Crasto, Victor Utz, Vijayanti Ramsaran, Vinita Ellerbe, Virginia Woodard, Wei Wei,

Welinson Kingsley, William Dolan, William Lopera, William Wallace, Winston Wynter, Yolanda Liu, and Zack Hiscock.

William Arthur Ward once said, "The mediocre teacher tells. The good teacher explains. The superior teacher demonstrates. The great teacher inspires." I have had the opportunity to work with more than 1,000 **great teachers** at NetCom Learning, some of whom I have listed here. Thank you all for teaching me so much about the importance of learning:

Adebayo Norman, Akash Bhatia, Akbar Khan, Alexis Valencia, Allan Jacobs, Amanda Govinda, Andrew Barnes, Andrew Gray, Andrew Ramdayal, Anthony Varriano, Aron Trauring, Arthur Brown, Arthur Gober, Beljulj Maskuli, Benjamin Moskovits, Bobby Lamaute, Bobby Williams, Brad Parker, Brian McClain, Bruce Robinson, Cari Maloney, Carmille Agana, Charles Hyman, Charles Williams, Charlie Lane, Christothea Gibbs, Clive Hermann, Daisy St. Mark, Daniel Bain, David Morgan, Denis Poloudin, Donald Fuller, Donnatella Craig, Emilio Grande-Garcia, Enayat Meer, Eric Ellison, Erick Polsky, Finnbarr Murphy, Frank Luo, Geeta Bhatia, Gene Plaskon, Ginger Myers, Glenn Harris, Ignacio Jimenez, Ilya Gindis, Jabari Garland, James Ring-Howell, Jeff Furman, Jeff Mullen, John Borhek, John Duhart, Joseph DeChiaro, Josh Penzell, Kalin Kirev, Kasi Prasad, Keith Charles, Kenneth Platt, Khalid El Harmassi, Larry Greenblatt, Manish Vaswani, Mark Ingram, Mark Lassoff, Michael Govinda, Michael Govinda Jr., Michael Zachensky, Mingya (Alan) Tang, Mohi Ahmed, Owen John, Patrick Loner, Paul Baxer, Paul Silva, Peter van Rossum, Pooja Parekh, Rafael Kemish, Ramesh Periasamy, Raul Aristy, Ray Holland, Richard Brown, Richard Govinda, Richard Landrigan, Richard Nyemb, Richard Oertle, Robert W. Dlouhy, Roger Mujica, Ronald Carroll, Rooz Kheirabi, Russell Sciurca, Sam Polsky, Sean Oriyano, Shelley L. Vinson, Sherwin Steele, Silas Jackson, Sohel Akhter, Tim Consolazio, Timothy Kaldis,

Todd Rosen, Victor Utz, Vijanti Ramsaran, Virginia Soyka, and William Dodson.

Michael LeBoeuf once said, "A satisfied customer is the best business strategy of all." With a team of dedicated and knowledgeable learning professionals, NetCom Learning has worked with more than 80 percent of the Fortune 100 companies and helped more than 10,000 organizations achieve their business goals. I want to thank some of those **customers** for helping me shape the innovative learning organization framework:

Amazon.com Inc., American International Group Inc., Automatic Data Processing Inc., Bank of America Corporation, Boeing Company, Booz Allen Hamilton, CACI International Inc., CenturyLink, Chevron Corporation, Cisco Systems Inc., Citigroup Inc., Comcast Corporation, Computer Sciences Corporation, Exelis Inc., 1199 National Benefit Fund for Health and Human Service Employees, American Broadcast Company Inc. (ABC), Asentus, Barclays Capital, Bloomberg L.P., Clark County School District, Columbia University, Continuum Health Partners, Credit Suisse, Delaware River Port Authority, Deloitte, Emerging Health Information Technology, Federal Bureau of Investigation (FBI), Federal Reserve System Fitch Ratings, Gardner Denver Inc., General Dynamics, Gogo, GS 1 US, Guardian Life Insurance Company, Hearst Corporation, Hewlett-Packard Company (HP), IBM, Internal Revenue Service (IRS), JPMorgan Chase, Joint Interagency Task Force South (JIATFS), Kirkwood Community College, Knowledge Consulting Group Inc., KnowledgePool, L-3 Communications, Latham & Watkins LLP, LearnSpectrum, Leviton Manufacturing, Lockheed Martin Corporation, McAllister Towing & Transportation, Metropolitan Transportation Authority (MTA): New York City Transit, Microsoft Corporation, MicroTek, Molina Medicaid Solutions–New Jersey, Morgan Stanley, Morpho Detection, Mount Sinai Health System, National Basketball

Association (NBA), National Institutes of Health (NIH), NES Associates, New York City Health and Hospitals Corporation (HHC), New York City Office of the Comptroller, New York Police Department (NYPD), New York Presbyterian Hospital, New York State Education Department Vocational and Educational Services for Individuals with Disabilities (VESID), Northrop Grumman Corporation, NYC Department of Citywide Administrative Services (DCAS), NYC Housing Authority, PEER 1 Hosting, PepsiCo, Pfizer Inc., Philadelphia Gas Works (PGW), Science Applications International Corporation (SAIC), SourceMedia Inc., Sunrise Technologies, The Rockefeller Group, Thomson Reuters, Time Warner Cable Inc., T-Mobile USA Inc., Touchbase USA Inc., Transport Workers Union (TWU) Local 100, NYC Transit Authority (NYCTA), Training & Upgrading Fund (TUF), UBS, United Nations, United Nations Children's Emergency Fund (UNICEF), United Parcel Service (UPS), United States Air Force, United States Army, United States Coast Guard, United States Marines, United States Navy, URS Corporation, U.S. Bureau of Indian Affairs (BIA), U.S. Department of Agriculture Food Safety and Inspection Service (USDA FSIS), U.S. Department of Defense, U.S. Department of Energy, U.S. Department of Homeland Security (DHS), U.S. Department of State, U.S. Department of the Interior (DOI), U.S. Department of Veterans Affairs (VA), Verizon Wireless, Wells Fargo & Company, and West Point Academy

I am grateful to work with **learning professionals** from the following companies. I am thankful for what I have learned from their research data, white papers, and blogs, and from the great learning conferences they have organized over the years:

Adobe Systems, Autodesk, Cisco Systems, Computing Technology Industry Association (CompTia), IBM, International Council of Electronic Commerce Consultants (EC-Council),

Microsoft Corporation, Oracle, Project Management Institute, Red Hat, and Sales Force.

These acknowledgements would not be complete without mentioning **my family**, who has always been my strength and support. To my **dad**—thank you for infusing me with the passion for learning. You are my mentor, coach, and hero. To my **mom**—thank you for your constant motivation and encouragement. You made me feel that I am number one and made me a confident person. To my **sister, Baby Apa**—thank you for teaching me math and chemistry. Watching you read every day helped me develop the passion for learning that has been so important in my life. To my older brother, **Mizan Bhai**—thank you for your support and encouragement throughout my life. To my younger brother, **Titu**—thank you for always being there for me. Finally, to my wife, **Therese**—I am deeply thankful to you for putting up with my crazy devotion to work-related projects, being my most helpful critic, and continuing to be my deepest, most supportive, and most enduring friend.

About the Author

RUSSELL SARDER is an award winning entrepreneur, author, and CEO of NetCom Learning. Under his leadership, NetCom Learning has become a multimillion-dollar business. In 2008 and 2011, *Inc* 5000 Magazine listed NetCom Learning as one of the fastest growing private companies in the United States.

A thought leader in the training industry, Sarder is the author of *Learning: Steps to Becoming a Passionate Lifelong Learner* and *Effective Learning Methods: How to Develop The Most Effective Learning Method.* He has been featured in *Yahoo! Finance*, CNBC, *Daily News*, and the *New York Times*; his television appearances include CBS Market Watch, and NY1. Sarder is also a business practitioner and mentor for MBA students and alumni at Columbia University.

Sarder was a winner of the 2011 Top Ten Asian American Business Awards and 50 Outstanding Asian Americans in Businesses. He is also the Chairman and CEO of Sarder Inc., a holding company that includes NetCom Learning, LearningGG, LearningCMS, Sarder Learning, Ebiz9, *Technology and Training* magazine, and other smaller companies. Microsoft Chairman Bill Gates, Microsoft CEO Steve Ballmer, and CISCO CEO John Chambers have contributed to his technology magazine.

A passionate believer in the value of lifelong learning, Sarder has undertaken various initiatives to multiply the impact of

NetCom Learning and reach those who have little or no opportunity to learn. NetCom has partnered with BRAC USA (Bangladesh Rural Advancement Committee) to help fund education for children in impoverished countries such as Bangladesh, South Sudan, Pakistan, and more. Each month NetCom awards the Sarder Scholarship, which provides $2,500 toward any NetCom Learning public or online class, to one driven individual wishing to begin or advance his or her IT career.

Index